# The My Little Pony G3 Collector's Inventory

by

## Summer Hayes

Priced Nostalgia Press ~ New Jersey

The information in this book is true and complete to the best of our knowledge. All information is made without any guarantee on the part of the author or publisher, who also disclaim any liability incurred in connection with the use of this guide.

We recognize that My Little Pony and all pony, set, and playset names are the exclusive property of Hasbro, Inc. and are used without permission. We are using them for identification purposes only. This is not an official publication, nor is it affiliated with Hasbro in any way. The toys featured in this book are from the private collection of the author and other collectors.

Additional copies of this book are available at www.PricedNostalgia.com.

Hayes, Summer. <u>The My Little Pony G3 Collector's Inventory: an Unofficial Full Color Illustrated Guide to the Third Generation of MLP Including All Ponies, Playsets and Accessories From 2003 to 2007</u>. 1st ed. New Jersey: Priced Nostalgia Press, 2007.

## About the Author

Summer Hayes has been a My Little Pony Collector for over twenty years. Her love of ponies started at a very early age and continued into her adult life. Over the years, she has accumulated an extensive collection of ponies, accessories, and merchandise from all three generations and from multiple countries. Summer has been active in the My Little Pony collecting community for many years and has attended pony meets and conventions throughout the country. Summer hosted My Little Pony Celebration: A Midwest Pony Meet in Greenville, Indiana in the summer of 2002 and co-hosted the event in Lafayette, Indiana in the summer of 2005. Summer is an elementary teacher and currently resides with her husband, Matthew, in Roanoke, Virginia.

## Special Thanks

Special thanks to my family for being so supportive of my obsession that is My Little Pony, my husband, Matt, for spending countless hours pony hunting, and Mary for hours of pony conversation.

For more information about Priced Nostalgia, additional titles on toy collecting and buying and selling on eBay, and to shop the collectibles in our store please visit us online at
**http://www.PricedNostalgia.com.**

My Little Pony collectors looking for additional resources, links, news, and places to buy, sell and trade MLP items should visit
**http://www.MyLittlePonyCollecting.com**

For other titles in the Collector's Inventory series, visit
**http://www.CollectorsInventory.com**

# Table of Contents

# Introduction

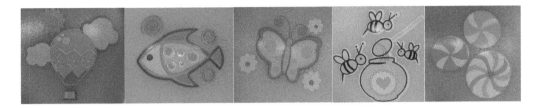

Since I can remember, My Little Pony toys have always been a part of my life. I have spent countless hours searching for missing pieces for my always-growing collection…and that isn't always the simplest of tasks. As with any collection, it can often be difficult to keep track of what you have and what you're seeking. Through my desire to categorize and keep my collection of G3 My Little Ponies as organized as possible, I created a resource that I hope will be helpful to new and old collectors alike.

This book contains information on the G3 My Little Pony line. The term G3 refers to Third Generation. Collectors commonly use the terms G1, G2, and G3 to signify to which release a pony belongs. G1, or First Generation, refers to ponies released in the early 1980's to the early 1990's. G2, or Second Generation, refers to ponies released between 1997 and 2003 and G3, or Third Generation, refers to ponies released after 2003. The G3 My Little Ponies are still currently available in stores at the time of printing.

G3 ponies have markings on one hip of their body known as a "cutie mark" or "symbol." These ponies also have a magnet in one hoof that activates special accessories as well as some playset features. In most instances, the foot with the magnet is marked with a small heart near the base of the pony's foot known as a "hoof heart."

The My Little Ponies in this book are organized according to the year and line in which they were released. Each year is then broken down into sets that are alphabetically listed. Playsets, Mail Order Ponies, So Soft Baby Ponies and other categories are listed in separate sections. A pony name index is provided in the back of this book to assist the reader when searching for a specific pony.

Each pony is pictured with an accompanying accessory checklist to help you organize your own collection. All ponies in this book were photographed immediately after being removed from their packaging. They were not styled, as I wished the photos to reflect their factory condition. Accessories are included in pony photographs and accessory colors are listed in most instances. However, I did not attempt to list brush colors since color names can sometimes be objective and all brushes clearly appear in the photographs.

I hope that you find this guide helpful while organizing your My Little Pony collection!

~Summer Hayes

# 2003
# My Little Pony
# Celebration

# Glitter Celebration Ponies
### (first set)

The initial set of Glitter Ponies was first available in the summer of 2003. They have pearly tinsel in their hair and were each boxed individually with a bow brush, charm, and a pearly ribbon. Each box was labeled with two Pony Points. (For more information about Pony Points, please see page 161)

☐ **Kimono** (lanterns)
　　☐ Bow brush
　　☐ Pinkish Purple charm and ribbon

☐ **Pinkie Pie** (balloons)
　　☐ Bow brush
　　☐ Pink charm and ribbon

☐ **Minty** (mints)
　　☐ Bow brush
　　☐ Mint green charm and ribbon

☐ **Sparkleworks** (fireworks)
　　☐ Bow brush
　　☐ Orange charm and ribbon

# Glitter Celebration Ponies
### (second set)

Two new Glitter Ponies were introduced in the fall of 2003 along with Sparkleworks and Pinkie Pie in new poses.

❑ **Sparkleworks II** (fireworks)
 ❑ Bow brush
 ❑ Orange charm and ribbon

❑ **Pinkie Pie II** (balloons)
 ❑ Bow brush
 ❑ Pink charm and ribbon

❑ **Strawberry Swirl** (strawberries and swirls)
 ❑ Bow brush
 ❑ Clear charm and ribbon

❑ **Daisyjo** (daisies)
 ❑ Bow brush
 ❑ Purple charm and ribbon

# Promotion Pack Ponies

Soon after the first G3 My Little Ponies hit the store shelves, Hasbro released promotional 2-packs, which included a free bonus pony packaged together with either Sparkleworks or Minty. The free ponies included Star Swirl, Autumn Skye, or Butterscotch. Promo sets that included Butterscotch were exclusively sold at Wal-Mart stores in the US. The free promo pony did not include a brush, charm, or ribbon in their packaging. However, these ponies were packaged as singles with accessories overseas.

❏ **Autumn Skye** (fall leaves)

❏ **Star Swirl** (glittery swirl)

❏ **Butterscotch** (lollipops)

In addition to the bonus pony promo packs, many ponies were packaged with a bonus A Charming Birthday video and a pink charm bracelet.

# Rainbow Celebration Ponies
### (first set)

The initial set of Rainbow Ponies was first available in the summer of 2003. Ponies in this set have multi-color hair and were each boxed individually with a bow brush, charm, and a pearly ribbon. Each box was labeled with two Pony Points.

- ❑ **Rainbow Dash** (rainbow and clouds)
  - ❑ Bow brush
  - ❑ Blue charm and ribbon

- ❑ **Wysteria** (flowers)
  - ❑ Bow brush
  - ❑ Violet charm and ribbon

- ❑ **Sunny Daze** (sun)
  - ❑ Bow brush
  - ❑ Clear charm and ribbon

- ❑ **Sweetberry** (strawberries)
  - ❑ Bow brush
  - ❑ Pink charm and ribbon

# Rainbow Celebration Ponies
### (second set)

Two new Rainbow Ponies were introduced in the fall of 2003 along with Rainbow Dash and Sunny Daze in new poses.

❐ **Rainbow Dash II** (rainbow and clouds)
   ❐ Bow brush
   ❐ Blue charm and ribbon

❐ **Sunny Daze II** (sun)
   ❐ Bow brush
   ❐ Clear charm and ribbon

❐ **Tink-a-Tink-a-Too** (bells)
   ❐ Bow brush
   ❐ Purple charm and ribbon

❐ **Fluttershy** (butterfly)
   ❐ Bow brush
   ❐ Pale pink charm and ribbon

# Seasons Ponies

The Seasons Ponies were sold throughout Europe and were packaged with a brush, charm, and ribbon. At the time of release, both Winter Snow and Sweet Summertime were European exclusives. Sweet Summertime would remain a European exclusive until 2005 when she was released in the Toys R Us Seaside Surprise with Sweet Summertime Accessory Playset. While Star Swirl and Butterscotch were not Seasons Ponies, they were sold with the seasons ponies in the Celebration assortment. Some European countries sold promotional packs containing a Seasons Pony and another pony.

❏ **Winter Snow** (snowflakes)
- ❏ Bow brush
- ❏ Pale blue charm

❏ **Sweet Summertime** (beach ball)
- ❏ Bow brush
- ❏ Melon charm

The following ponies are also included in this assortment, but are not pictured (please see Promotion Pack Ponies section for photographs of these ponies).

❏ **Autumn Sky** (fall leaves)
- ❏ Bow brush
- ❏ Charm and ribbon

❏ **Butterscotch** (lollipops)
- ❏ Gold bow brush
- ❏ Gold charm and ribbon

❏ **Star Swirl** (glittery swirl)
- ❏ White bow brush
- ❏ Clear pony charm and ribbon

❏ **Spring Fever** (flowers)
- ❏ Bow brush
- ❏ Pink charm

# Winter Ponies
### (first set)

In winter of 2003, a set of three winter-themed ponies was released. Each pony had a winter themed "cutie mark," and was packaged in a box decorated with snowflakes with a brush, and winter accessories. This set was sold exclusively in Target stores within the US and Australia. The winter ponies were packaged four to a shipping carton with one Snowflake, one Candy Cane, and two Mittens ponies. Thus, Mittens is the most common.

❑ **Snowflake** (snowflake)
    ❑ Bow brush
    ❑ Winter hat

❑ **Candy Cane** (candy cane and holly)
    ❑ Bow brush
    ❑ Santa hat

❑ **Mittens** (pine tree and snowflakes)
    ❑ Bow brush
    ❑ 4 mittens
    ❑ Scarf

# Accessory Packs

These sets consisted of a pony or ponies and various themed accessories. These accessory packs were called "Slice of Life" sets. Picnic Celebration was a Toys R Us exclusive and Tea Party was a KB toys exclusive, while both Birthday Celebration and Moonlight Celebration sets were available at most retailers.

**Moonlight Celebration with Moondancer**
- ☐ **Moondancer** (moon and stars)
    - ☐ Boom box
    - ☐ Sleeping blanket
    - ☐ Teddy bear
    - ☐ 4 bunny slippers
    - ☐ Bottle of soda
    - ☐ 2 cups
    - ☐ Bowl of Popcorn
    - ☐ Cell phone
    - ☐ 2 curlers
    - ☐ Blue comb
    - ☐ Blue charm and ribbon

**Birthday Celebration Razzaroo**
- ☐ **Razzaroo** (present)
    - ☐ Birthday cake with candle
    - ☐ 4 slices of cake
    - ☐ 4 forks
    - ☐ Gift box
    - ☐ Candy tray (fits inside gift box)
    - ☐ Purple tray
    - ☐ Purple comb
    - ☐ Purple charm and ribbon

## Picnic Celebration with Applejack (TRU exclusive)

- ❏ **Applejack** (apple)
- ❏ Vinyl apple backpack
- ❏ Picnic basket
- ❏ Tree Trunk with raccoon
- ❏ 3 double apples
- ❏ 3 sandwiches on plates
- ❏ 3 forks and knives with napkins
- ❏ 3 cups
- ❏ Soda bottle
- ❏ Pie
- ❏ 1 piece of pie on serving utensil
- ❏ Green apple brush with decal
- ❏ Pale orange-pink charm and ribbon

## Tea Party (KB toys exclusive)

- ❏ **Spring Fever** (flowers)
- ❏ **Applejack** (apple)
- ❏ Vinyl carry case
- ❏ Teapot
- ❏ Sugar bowl
- ❏ Creamer
- ❏ 3 Teacups
- ❏ 3 Saucers
- ❏ Green apple brush
- ❏ Pink bow brush

# 2004
# Friendship Ball

# Eveningwear Fashions

These ponies came dressed ready to attend the friendship ball. Sparkleworks and Sunny Daze were produced in new poses and two new store exclusive ponies were introduced.

## Eveningwear with Sparkleworks

❑ **Sparkleworks III** (fireworks)
- ❑ Purple bow brush
- ❑ Purple crown
- ❑ Ruffled skirt
- ❑ Purple barrette
- ❑ 4 purple shoes

## Eveningwear with Sunny Daze

❑ **Sunny Daze III** (sun)
- ❑ Pink pearly bow brush
- ❑ Pink pearly crown
- ❑ Sequined cape
- ❑ Flower hair band
- ❑ 4 pink shoes

**Eveningwear with Crystal Lake**

☐ **Crystal Lake** (Target Exclusive) (starburst)
- ☐ Purple bow brush*
- ☐ Heart pendant necklace
- ☐ White ruffled skirt
- ☐ Pink purse
- ☐ Purple barrette*

*This pony was also sold with an orange brush and orange barrette

**Eveningwear with Wind Wisher**

☐ **Wind Wisher** (Toys R Us exclusive) (pinwheels)
- ☐ Pink bow brush
- ☐ Purple crown
- ☐ Light blue dress
- ☐ Purple barrette

# Glitter Ponies
### (third and fourth sets)

In 2004, Daisyjo and Strawberry Swirl were reissued without charms and with different backcard pictures. Two new ponies, Serendipity and Bumblesweet, were introduced in this assortment. Some ponies in this assortment were packaged with 30 bonus stickers. Another assortment of Glitter Ponies was issued in the spring, containing both Serendipity and Bumblesweet along with Cupcake and Sweetsong. Both Cupcake and Sweetsong were hard to find in stores during this time. Eventually, they were offered in shrink-wrapped packages at Wal-Mart stores and were easier for collectors to locate.

❑ **Serendipity** (four-leaf clovers)
  ❑ Bow brush

❑ **Bumblesweet** (bees and a honey pot)
  ❑ Bow brush

❑ **Cupcake** (cupcakes)
  ❑ Bow brush

❑ **Sweetsong** (mandolin)
  ❑ Bow brush

# Jewel Ponies
**(first set)**

Jewel Ponies have glittery jewels as their symbols.

☐ **Gem Blossom** (jeweled flower)
    ☐ Flower brush

☐ **Valenshy** (jeweled heart)
    ☐ Flower brush

☐ **Crystal Lace** (jeweled lace)
    ☐ Flower brush

☐ **Peri Winkle** (jeweled design)
    ☐ Flower brush

# Jewel Ponies
**(second set)**

The second set of Jewel Ponies was available in the fall of 2004. Jewel Ponies have glittery jewels as their symbols.

❑ **Sapphire Shores** (jeweled shell)
   ❑ Flower brush

❑ **Wondermint** (jeweled leaves)
   ❑ Flower brush

❑ **Star Dasher** (jeweled star)
   ❑ Flower brush

# Jewel and Sparkle Ponies
### (Target Exclusives)

In 2004, Target sold two Jewel Ponies and two Sparkle Ponies that were store exclusives.

❏ **Winterberry** (jeweled design)
  ❏ Flower brush

❏ **Juniper Jade** (jeweled design)
  ❏ Flower brush

❏ **Blue Mist** (glitter swirls)
  ❏ Bow brush

❏ **Savannah Sage** (glitter heart and design)
  ❏ Bow brush

# Perfectly Pony
**(first set)**

The first Perfectly Pony set was available in most stores during the summer of 2004. Perfectly Ponies were a combined set of Rainbow Ponies and Glitter Ponies. Each pony was packaged with a brush.

❏ **Skywishes** (kite and a butterfly)
    ❏ Bow brush

❏ **Bee Bop** (harp and music notes)
    ❏ Bow brush

❏ **Sunset Sweety** (flowers and stems)
    ❏ Bow brush

❏ **Triple Treat** (lollipop, ice cream, and cookie)
    ❏ Bow brush

# Perfectly Pony
**(second set)**

This set of Perfectly Ponies was available in the fall of 2004. The characters in this group were also available as part of Disney's Once Upon a Toy "Build a Pony Workshop" (see Disney Ponies section for more information).

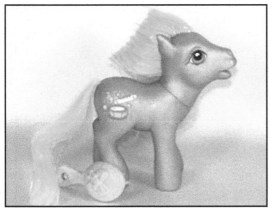

☐ **Piccolo** (piccolo, drum, and music notes)
    ☐ Bow brush

☐ **Cinnamon Breeze** (cinnamon bun)
    ☐ Bow brush

☐ **Spring Parade** (flowers)
    ☐ Bow brush

☐ **Golden Delicious** (heart and apple)
    ☐ Bow brush

# Pretty Pony Fashions

These ponies were dressed in adorable outfits and often included small themed accessories. Both Butterscotch and Star Swirl were in their original poses, but Pinkie Pie and Rainbow Dash were produced in yet another pose. Royal Ribbon and Tea Leaf were sold as store exclusives at Target and Toys R Us respectively.

**Berry Pickin' Fun with Butterscotch**
- ❏ **Butterscotch** (lollipops)
    - ❏ Yellow flower brush
    - ❏ Floral print hat
    - ❏ Floral print skirt
    - ❏ Basket
    - ❏ Blueberries
    - ❏ Strawberries

**Rain or Shine Garden Time with Star Swirl**
- ❏ **Star Swirl** (glittery swirl)
    - ❏ Bright pink flower brush
    - ❏ Pink rain hat
    - ❏ Pink rain coat
    - ❏ Watering can
    - ❏ Gardening pot
    - ❏ 2 flower bouquets

**Pie Party with Pinkie Pie**
- ❏ **Pinkie Pie III** (balloons)
    - ❏ Pink flower brush
    - ❏ Floral headpiece
    - ❏ Floral skirt
    - ❏ Pie
    - ❏ Pie server with pie piece
    - ❏ 2 sandwiches

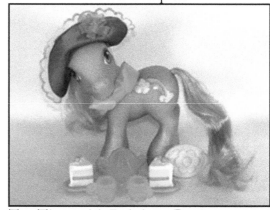

**Tea Time with Rainbow Dash**
- ❏ **Rainbow Dash III** (rainbow and clouds)
    - ❏ Blue flower brush
    - ❏ Purple satin hat
    - ❏ Pink neck bow
    - ❏ Teapot
    - ❏ 2 teacups
    - ❏ 2 pieces of cake

❏ **Royal Ribbon (Target exclusive)** (damsel hat)
  ❏ Bow brush
  ❏ Pink damsel hat
  ❏ Pink cape

❏ **Tea Leaf (Toys R Us exclusive)** (teacup)
  ❏ Blue comb
  ❏ Yellow bathrobe
  ❏ Blue eye mask
  ❏ Pink teddy bear
  ❏ 4 yellow bunny slippers

# Rainbow Ponies
## (third and fourth sets)

In 2004, Fluttershy and Tink-a-Tink-a-Too were reissued without charms and with different backcard pictures. Two new ponies, Sew-and So and Toola-Roola were introduced in this assortment. Some ponies in this assortment were packaged with 30 bonus stickers. Another assortment of Rainbow Ponies was issued in the spring, containing both Toola-Roola and Sew-and So along with Shenanigans and Cherry Blossom. Both Shenanigans and Cherry Blossom were hard to find in stores during this time. Eventually, they began showing up at discount chains during the late summer months.

❒ **Sew-and-So** (button and hearts)
   ❒ Bow brush

❒ **Toola-Roola** (swirls and hearts)
   ❒ Bow brush

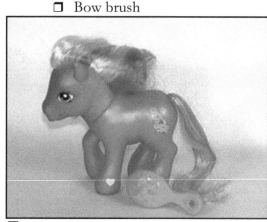

❒ **Shenanigans** (hot air balloon)
   ❒ Bow brush

❒ **Cherry Blossom** (flowers)
   ❒ Bow brush

# Sparkle Ponies
**(first set)**

Sparkle Ponies have glitter on their symbols and foreheads.

❑ **Starbeam** (glitter shooting stars)
   ❑ Bow brush

❑ **Desert Rose** (glitter rose)
   ❑ Bow brush

❑ **Forsythia** (glitter flowers and butterfly)
   ❑ Bow brush

❑ **Merriweather** (glitter umbrella)
   ❑ Bow brush

# Sparkle Ponies
**(second set)**

A second set of Sparkle Ponies were released later in the year.

☐ **Desert Blossom** (glitter cactus)
  ☐ Bow brush

☐ **Rainbow Swirl** (glitter sundae)
  ☐ Bow brush

☐ **Denim Blue** (glitter pocket with flowers)
  ☐ Bow brush

☐ **Peachy Pie** (glitter peach and flower)
  ☐ Bow brush

# Spring/Easter Ponies
## (Target Exclusive)

In the spring of 2004, Target stores sold three store exclusive spring/Easter themed ponies. These ponies were packaged on a bubble card with an egg shaped bubble. Each came wearing a cloth bonnet.

❑ **Toodleloo** (Easter eggs)
    ❑ Purple polka dot/floral hat
    ❑ Bow brush

❑ **Doseydotes** (butterfly)
    ❑ Orange floral hat
    ❑ Bow brush

❑ **Spring Treat** (tulips)
    ❑ Pastel polka dot/striped hat
    ❑ Bow brush

# Super Long-Hair Ponies with Babies

Super Long-Hair Ponies have extra long hair. Each Super Long-Hair Pony came packaged with a brush, crown, and barrette. Some were packaged with a bonus baby pony. Both Petal Blossom and Rainbow Flash were packaged individually and with a bonus baby pony.

❏ **Petal Blossom** (flowers)
With Bonus Baby Flower Flash
- ❏ Bow brush
- ❏ Pink crown
- ❏ Green flower barrette with colored ribbons
- ❏ Green flower barrette with pearly ribbons

❏ **Rainbow Flash** (rainbow, cloud, and sun)
With Bonus Baby Romperooni
- ❏ Bow brush
- ❏ Purple crown
- ❏ Purple flower barrette with colored ribbons
- ❏ Purple flower barrette with pearly ribbons

❏ **Aloha Pearl (Toys R Us Exclusive)** (tropical flowers)
With Bonus Baby Bellaluna
- ❏ Bow brush
- ❏ Pink crown
- ❏ Green flower barrette with colored ribbons
- ❏ Green flower barrette with pearly ribbons

❏ **Wing Song Target Exclusive** (butterfly)
With Bonus Baby Goody Gumdrop
- ❏ Bow brush
- ❏ Pink crown
- ❏ Purple flower barrette with colored ribbons
- ❏ Purple flower barrette with pearly ribbons

Baby Flower Flash and Baby Romperooni were not originally named when they were packaged with the Super Long-Hair Ponies. Both were named in later years upon their reissue. (Baby Flower Flash was named when she was packaged as a bonus baby with the Musical Wishes Jewelry Box and Baby Romperooni was named when she was packaged with the second edition of Celebration Castle.)

❑ **Baby Flower Flash** (flowers)
Packaged with Petal Blossom

❑ **Baby Romperooni** (flowers)
Packaged with Rainbow Flash

❑ **Baby Bellaluna** (baby bottle and rattle)
Packaged with Aloha Pearl

❑ **Baby Goody Gumdrop** (gumdrops on pink)
Packaged with Wing Song

# Super Long-Hair Ponies

Three new Super Long-Hair Ponies were introduced later in 2004. These included Silly Sunshine, Silver Song, and Sparklesnap. Sparklesnap was a Toys R Us exclusive.

❏ **Silly Sunshine** (dragonfly and daisies)
    ❏ Green flower barrette
        with colored ribbons
    ❏ Bow brush

❏ **Silver Song** (theatrical masks and music notes)
    ❏ Purple flower barrette
        with colored ribbons
    ❏ Bow brush

❏ **Sparklesnap (Toys R Us exclusive)**
    ❏ Yellow flower barrette with colored ribbons
    ❏ Yellow flower barrette with pearly ribbons
    ❏ Bow brush

# Target Exclusive 3-Pack

During the fall of 2004, Target stores carried two store exclusive 3-packs. These 3-packs contained two rainbow ponies and a baby pony. One pack contained Sew-and-So (reissue), Tink-a-Tink-a-Too (reissue), and Baby Keen Bean. The other pack contained Fluttershy (reissue), Toola-Roola (reissue), and Baby Pink Sunsparkle (reissue).

❏ **Sew-and-So** (button and hearts)
❏ **Tink-a-Tink-a-Too** (bells)
❏ **Baby Keen Bean** (beans)
  ❏ brush
  ❏ brush

❏ **Fluttershy** (butterfly)
❏ **Toola-Roola** (swirls and hearts)
❏ **Baby Pink Sunsparkle**
(shining heart inside a heart)
  ❏ brush
  ❏ brush

❏ **Baby Keen Bean** (close-up)

# Twirling Fun with Loop-De-La and Ice Dancing with Glitter Glide

The Twirling Fun with Loop-de-La and Ice Dancing with Glitter Glide sets contained a pony with a light-up tiara, a spinning stand, and a variety of accessories. These sets were later sold at Wal-Mart stores with a bonus pony. Glitter Glide was packaged with Minty II, who was in a new pose, and Loop-De-La was packaged with Sparkleworks II. Later, both of these ponies were found in Walgreen's stores packaged with a bonus Baby Goody Gumdrop. Both Glitter Glide and Loop-De-La have jointed necks and waists so they can be posed to dance.

Close-up of Loop-De-La

☐ **Loop-De-La** (ballet slippers and flowers)
- ☐ 2-piece pedestal (pink)
- ☐ Pink tutu
- ☐ 2 removable ballet slippers
- ☐ Purple flower bouquet
- ☐ Bow brush

Close-up of Glitter Glide

☐ **Glitter Glide** (ice skates and snowflakes)
- ☐ 2 piece pedestal (blue/green)
- ☐ Blue tutu
- ☐ 2 removable ice skates
- ☐ Pink flower bouquet
- ☐ Bow brush

❑ **Minty II** (bonus pony packaged with Glitter Glide) (mints)

Twirling Fun with Loop-De-La
shown packaged alone.

Ice Dancing with Glitter Glide shown with bonus pony
packaging that was available at Wal-Mart stores.

# Winter Ponies

In winter of 2004, a second set of three winter-themed ponies was released. Each pony had a winter themed cutie mark, and was packaged in a box decorated with snowflakes with a brush and winter accessories. This set was sold exclusively in Target stores within the US and Australia. The winter ponies were packaged four to a shipping carton with one Marshmellow Coco, one Mistletoe, and two Snow'el ponies. Thus, Snow'el is the most common.

❑ **Marshmellow Coco** (coco, saucer, and cookies)
  - ❑ Winter hat
  - ❑ Tail bow
  - ❑ Bow brush

❑ **Mistletoe** (holiday ornaments)
  - ❑ Santa hat
  - ❑ Holiday light ribbon necklace
  - ❑ Bow brush

❒ **Snow'el** (mittens)
- ❒ Fuzzy earmuffs
- ❒ Fuzzy boots
- ❒ Stripped scarf
- ❒ Bow brush

# Accessory Packs

In 2004, there were many new pony and accessory sets available. Many of these sets were store exclusives. In addition to new sets, Birthday Celebration with Razzaroo and Moonlight Celebration with Moondancer sets were reissued in slightly different packaging and without their pony charms.

**Dance Jamboree with Blossomforth**

Blossomforth with her outfit removed

❑ **Blossomforth** (3 flowers)
- ❑ Blue skirt
- ❑ Blue boa
- ❑ 4 Dance shoes
- ❑ Glasses
- ❑ Hair barrette
- ❑ Hair band
- ❑ Bow brush

The Wishing Well Princess Playset was found exclusively at KB toys in the US, but was found at multiple retailers in other parts of the world. The Port-o-Bella and Lickety Split set was a Kmart exclusive within the US.

## Wishing Well Princess Playset
- ☐ **Crystal Crown** (crown )
  - ☐ Damsel Hat
  - ☐ Cape
  - ☐ Wishing Well
  - ☐ Special brush

## Port-o-Bella and Lickety Split
- ☐ **Port-o-Bella** (mushroom)
- ☐ **Lickety Split** (sundae)
  - ☐ Polka dotted hat
  - ☐ Striped  ice cream hat
  - ☐ Picnic basket
  - ☐ 3 sandwiches
  - ☐ 3 napkins
  - ☐ Pie
  - ☐ Pie server
  - ☐ Beverage bottle
  - ☐ 3 glasses
  - ☐ Bow brush
  - ☐ Bow brush

Butterfly Surprise with Avalonia was sold exclusively at Toys R Us stores.

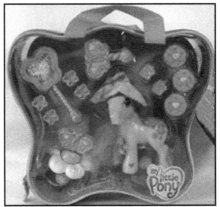

**Butterfly Surprise with Avalonia**
- ❑ **Avalonia** (Butterfly with three flowers)
    - ❑ Twirling Butterfly on a flower
    - ❑ Butterfly net
    - ❑ Hat
    - ❑ 3 jars
    - ❑ 2 butterfly barrettes
    - ❑ 4 Butterflies
    - ❑ Butterfly brush

Butterfly Surprise with Avalonia came packaged in a cute butterfly carrying case.

Ponyville Tea Party was sold exclusively at Costco stores in a clear backpack. This set can be somewhat difficult to find. All four ponies included in this set are reissues, but they contain slight variations. For example, Sunset Sweety is a darker shade than in her original release.

**Ponyville Tea Party**
- ❑ **Skywishes** (kite and a butterfly)
- ❑ **Beebop** (harp and music notes)
- ❑ **Sunset Sweety** (flowers and stems)
- ❑ **Triple Treat** (lollipop, ice cream, and cookie)
    - ❑ Teapot
    - ❑ Sugar bowl
    - ❑ Creamer
    - ❑ 3 Teacups
    - ❑ 3 Saucers
    - ❑ Mirror
    - ❑ Pink glittery cape
    - ❑ Pink satin hat
    - ❑ Blue raincoat
    - ❑ Blue rain hat
    - ❑ Blue dotted skirt
    - ❑ Pink dotted hat
    - ❑ 4 bow brushes

# Spring Basket

The Spring Basket contained three ponies and multiple accessories packaged in a bucket made to look like a basket. The accessories included in this set came in a variety of colors. In other words, the color of individual parts (such as the watering can) can vary in color from set to set.

❐ **Bubblecup** (bubble dish and bubble wand)

❐ **Garden Glade** (flower inside a circle)

❐ **Wishawhirl** (pinwheels)

**Spring Basket Accessories**

# Special Ponies and Packs

Several ponies were released in 2004 that did not belong to any certain set. This section is designated to feature these ponies.

### Pepperberry
☐ **Pepperberry**
(pepper shaker, strawberry and swirls)
☐ Bow brush

Pepperberry was available exclusively at KB toy stores. She was used as part of a promotional offer in the store and was also available for sale at some stores.

### Star Shimmer
☐ **Star Shimmer** (starburst)
☐ Flower brush

Star Shimmer was exclusive to Toys R Us stores. When you purchased Star Shimmer, a $1 donation was made to the Starlight Children's Foundation. This organization is a non-profit organization serving seriously ill children and their families.

## Sunshower and Luau

- ☐ **Sunshower** (sun, cloud and rain)
- ☐ **Luau** (hibiscus flower)
    - ☐ Flower brush
    - ☐ Flower brush

This set was available exclusively at Wal-Mart stores. This set came packaged in a plastic tote with a clear front. Both of these ponies are Super Long-Hair ponies.

## Pick-a-Lily and Sunny Salsa

- ☐ **Pick-a-Lilly** (lily)
- ☐ **Sunny Salsa** (circle and flower design)
    - ☐ Yellow raincoat
    - ☐ Yellow rain hat
    - ☐ Bright pink frilly skirt
    - ☐ Pink Crown
    - ☐ Bow brush
    - ☐ Bow brush

Pick-a-Lily and Sunny Salsa without their outfits.

❏ **Star Catcher**
(glittery heart with tiny stars)
    ❏ Dancing in the Clouds VHS video
    ❏ Purple crown
    ❏ Bow brush

Star Catcher was the first Pegasus pony available in the G3 line. Star Catcher is unique to later released Pegasus ponies because she has fabric wings instead of molded wings.

My Little Pony PC Play Pack
❏ **Sparkleberry Swirl** (swirls and stars)
    ❏ My Little Pony PC Game
Hasbro conducted on online vote to determine the name of this pony on the official MLP website.

# Toys R Us 4-Pack

This 4-Pack was available exclusively at Toys R Us stores. It included four new ponies and was available in time for the 2004 holiday season.

❑ **Flutterbutter** (wings)
    ❑ Bow brush

❑ **Princess Peppermint**
(crown and peppermint sticks)
    ❑ Bow brush

❑ **Banjo Blue** (banjo)
    ❑ Bow brush

❑ **Tropical Delight** (tropical flowers)
    ❑ Bow brush

Mint in box Toys R Us 4-Pack

# 2005
# Butterfly Island

# Dazzle Bright Ponies

Dazzle Bright Ponies have brightly colored bodies and hair. The first set of four Dazzle Bright Ponies arrived on store shelves in early 2005. Coconut Cream and Ribbon Wishes were released shortly after.

❒ **Beachberry** (tropical flower)
  ❒ Flower brush

❒ **Bowtie** (bows)
  ❒ Flower brush

❒ **Kiwi Tart** (key lime pie)
  ❒ Flower brush

❒ **Sea Spray** (starfish)
  ❒ Flower brush

❒ **Coconut Cream** (coconut cream pie)   ❒ **Ribbon Wishes** (star wand)
    ❒ Flower brush          ❒ Flower brush

# Discount Ponies

This set of ponies was a little difficult to place because they don't have an official name for their set. They were sold at discount chains throughout the US including Family Dollar stores, Big Lots stores, and Value City stores. When they were originally discovered, collectors referred to them as "Family Dollar Ponies." These four adult ponies were sold on small cards similar to Pepperberry and the Target Exclusive baby ponies. Each pony came packaged with a brush.

❑ Autumn Crisp (pumpkin, corn stalks, leaves)
    ❑ Bow brush

❑ Misty Blue (flowers)
    ❑ Bow brush

❑ Peachie Keen (peaches and flowers)
    ❑ Bow brush

❑ Strawberry Sunset (strawberries)
    ❑ Bow brush

# Dream Design Ponies
## (first set)

Dream Design Ponies have three dimensional raised symbols.

❏ **Island Delight** (seashell and heart)
  ❏ Flower brush

❏ **Paradise Palms** (daisy)
  ❏ Flower brush

❏ **Sand Dollar** (sand dollar)
  ❏ Flower brush

❏ **Seascape** (sun)
  ❏ Flower brush

# Dream Design Ponies
## (second set)

A second set of Dream Design Ponies was released in late 2005.

☐ **Beachcomber** (tropical flower)
    ☐ Flower brush

☐ **Cloud Climber** (butterfly)
    ☐ Flower brush

☐ **Desert Palm** (palm trees)
    ☐ Flower brush

☐ **Summer Berry** (grapes)
    ☐ Flower brush

# Dress-up Daywear Ponies

Dress-up Daywear Ponies came packaged with outfits and accessories.

❐ **Bubble Bath Time with Sweetsong (II)**
(mandolin)
- ❐ Robe
- ❐ Hair towel
- ❐ Powder puff
- ❐ Rubber duckie
- ❐ Bubble bath
- ❐ 2 curlers
- ❐ Bow brush

❐ **Study Break with Shenanigans (II)**
(hot air balloon)
- ❐ School outfit
- ❐ Beret
- ❐ Satchel
- ❐ Book
- ❐ Apples
- ❐ Bracelet
- ❐ Bow brush

❐ **Whimsical Winter with Pinkie Pie (II)**
(balloons)
- ❐ Skirt
- ❐ Crown
- ❐ 4 ice skates
- ❐ Star barrette
- ❐ Bow brush

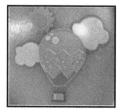

Close- up symbol pictures of Sweet Song, Shenanigans, and Pinkie Pie

# Dress-up Daywear Wing Wishes Ponies

These ponies came dressed in butterfly outfits. They were all packaged individually as well as with a bonus pony except for Wing Wishes Blossomforth.  She was available exclusively at Toys R Us stores packaged with bonus Spring Fever.

❑ **Wing Wishes with Blossomforth (TRU exclusive)** (flowers)
- ❑ Butterfly wings
- ❑ Antenna headpiece
- ❑ Wand
- ❑ Bracelet
- ❑ Bow brush

❑ **Wing Wishes with Fluttershy (II)** (butterfly and flowers)
- ❑ Butterfly Wings
- ❑ Antenna headpiece
- ❑ Wand
- ❑ Bracelet
- ❑ Bow brush

❑ **Wing Wishes with Minty (III)**
(mints)

- ❑ Butterfly wings
- ❑ Antenna headpiece
- ❑ Wand
- ❑ Bracelet
- ❑ Bow brush

❑ **Wing Wishes with Toola-Roola (II)**
(swirls and hearts)

- ❑ Butterfly wings
- ❑ Antenna headpiece
- ❑ Wand
- ❑ Bracelet
- ❑ Bow brush

Close- up symbol pictures of Blossomforth, Fluttershy, Minty, and Toola-Roola.

Dress-up Daywear Wing Wishes bonus packages contained ponies that had been previously released.

Wing Wishes Blossomforth was packaged
with bonus Spring Fever

Wing Wishes Fluttershy was packaged
with bonus Doseydotes

Wing Wishes Minty was packaged
with bonus Tea Leaf

Wing Wishes Toola-Roola was packaged
with bonus Meadowbrook

# Fun with Ponies

These sets were sold at discount stores within the US. They contain re-released ponies and accessories.

**Dress-Up Fun with Skywishes**
- ❏ **Skywishes** (kite and a butterfly)
    - ❏ Skirt
    - ❏ Necklace
    - ❏ Purse
    - ❏ Bow brush

**Picnic Fun with Sew-and-So**
- ❏ **Sew-and-So** (button and hearts)
    - ❏ Picnic basket
    - ❏ 2 sandwiches
    - ❏ 2 silverware sets
    - ❏ 2 cups
    - ❏ Soda bottle
    - ❏ Bow brush

**Tea Time with Piccolo**
- ❏ **Piccolo** (piccolo, drum, and music notes)
    - ❏ Hat
    - ❏ Teapot
    - ❏ 2 teacups
    - ❏ 2 saucers
    - ❏ 2 pieces of cake
    - ❏ Bow brush

# Jewel Birthday Ponies

Jewel Birthday Ponies were sold exclusively at Toys R Us stores. There are twelve ponies in this set (one pony for each month of the year). Jewel Birthday Ponies have a jeweled-colored birthstone symbol that matches the pony's month.

❏ **January Joy** (garnet party hat and blower)
    ❏ Flower brush

❏ **Fantastical February**
(amethyst flower and heart design)
    ❏ Flower brush

❏ **March Mischief** (aquamarine teacup)
    ❏ Flower brush

❏ **April Mist** (diamond umbrella)
    ❏ Flower brush

❏ **May Belle** (emerald flower)
    ❏ Flower brush

❏ **June Blossom** (alexandrite butterfly)
    ❏ Flower brush

❏ **July Jubilee** (ruby raspberry)
   ❏ Flower brush

❏ **August Breeze** (peridot shell)
   ❏ Flower brush

❏ **Sweet September** (sapphire flowers)
   ❏ Flower brush

❏ **October Dreams** (tourmaline flower)
   ❏ Flower brush

❏ **November Nights** (topaz flower and leaves)
   ❏ Flower brush

❏ **December Delight** (turquoise bow)
   ❏ Flower brush

# Perfectly Pony
### (third set)

More ponies were released under the category of "Perfectly Pony" in 2005.

☐ **Gardenia Glow** (gardenia flowers)
    ☐ Flower brush

☐ **Heather Winds** (butterfly and flowers)
    ☐ Flower brush

☐ **Magic Marigold**
(top hat, marigolds, and cane)
    ☐ Flower brush

☐ **Sweet Breeze** (cloud and flowers)
    ☐ Flower brush

# Perfectly Pony
**(fourth set)**

Yet another set of "Perfectly Ponies" appeared in mid-2005 including a jewel pony, Twilight Twinkle.

❑ **Alphabittle** (alphabet soup)
   ❑ Flower brush

❑ **Bunches-o-Fun** (bouquet of flowers)
   ❑ Flower brush

❑ **Fair Weather** (puffy clouds)
   ❑ Flower brush

❑ **Twilight Twinkle** (jewel flower/star)
   ❑ Flower brush

# Ponies on the Go

Who thought that ponies would ever have their own scooters? This set not only provided ponies with a speedy way to get around, but also all the accessories necessary for scooter fun. These ponies were widely available at most retailers, with the exception of Flitter Flutter, who was a Target exclusive.

☐ **Breezie** (tree blowing in the wind)
- ☐ Scooter
- ☐ Helmet
- ☐ Flag
- ☐ Satchel
- ☐ Water bottle
- ☐ Apples
- ☐ Map
- ☐ Bow brush

☐ **Scooter Sprite** (scooter)
- ☐ Scooter
- ☐ Helmet
- ☐ Flag
- ☐ Satchel
- ☐ Camera
- ☐ Cell phone
- ☐ Map
- ☐ Bow brush

☐ **Bumbleberry** (berry)
- ☐ Scooter
- ☐ Helmet
- ☐ Flag
- ☐ Backpack
- ☐ Lunch box
- ☐ Strawberries
- ☐ Comb
- ☐ Bow brush

☐ **Scootaloo** (butterfly)
- ☐ Scooter
- ☐ Helmet
- ☐ Flag
- ☐ Backpack
- ☐ Jar
- ☐ 2 butterfly hairclips
- ☐ Comb
- ☐ Bow brush

☐ **Flitter Flutter (Target Exclusive)**

    ☐ Scooter
    ☐ Helmet
    ☐ Flag
    ☐ Satchel
    ☐ Camera
    ☐ Cell phone
    ☐ Bow brush

# Ponies with Bonus Baby

These sets were made up of repackaged ponies and were available at discount chains such as Family Dollar stores and Value City stores.

❐ **Pinkie Pie** (balloons)
❐ **Bellaluna** (rattle)
    ❐ Bow brush

❐ **Toola-Roola** (swirls and hearts)
❐ **Goody Gumdrop** (gumdrops)
    ❐ Bow brush

The Meadowbrook and Flower Flash set is not pictured. Please see Bloomin' Blossoms playset section for pictures of Meadowbrook and Super Long-Hair Ponies with Babies section for pictures of Flower Flash

# Pony and Me

These sets contained a pony and fun accessories.

**Let's Go with Strawberry Swirl**
- ❏ **Strawberry Swirl** (strawberries and swirls)
    - ❏ Purse
    - ❏ Pony-sized purse
    - ❏ Magazine
    - ❏ Pony-sized magazine
    - ❏ Bow brush

**Sharing Tea with Serendipity**
- ❏ **Serendipity** (four-leafed clover)
    - ❏ Teapot
    - ❏ Creamer
    - ❏ 2 teacups
    - ❏ 2 saucers
    - ❏ 2 small teacups
    - ❏ 2 small saucers
    - ❏ Bow brush

**Sunny Adventures with Blossomforth**
- ❏ **Blossomforth (II)** (three flowers)
    - ❏ Purse
    - ❏ Pony-sized purse
    - ❏ Glasses (cardboard)
    - ❏ Pony-sized glasses
    - ❏ Flower brush

**Sweet Adventures with Triple Treat**
- ❏ **Triple Treat (II)**
(lollypop, ice cream and cookie)
    - ❏ Purse
    - ❏ Pony-sized purse
    - ❏ Magazine with stickers
    - ❏ Pony-sized magazine
    - ❏ Flower brush

# Seaside Celebration Ponies
### (first set)

The Seaside Celebration Ponies are all ready for a day at the beach. These ponies were sold individually within the U.S., but were packaged with a bonus baby pony in some countries.

❑ **Bumblesweet (II)** (bees and a honey pot)
   - ❑ Swimsuit
   - ❑ Towel
   - ❑ Glasses
   - ❑ Radio
   - ❑ Sun tan lotion
   - ❑ Hair barrette
   - ❑ Bow brush

❑ **Cherry Blossom (II)** (flowers)
   - ❑ Swimsuit
   - ❑ Towel
   - ❑ Glasses
   - ❑ Beach bag
   - ❑ Water bottle
   - ❑ Cell phone
   - ❑ Bow brush

❏ **Wysteria (II)** (flowers)
- ❏ Sundress
- ❏ Sandcastle
- ❏ Glasses
- ❏ Pail
- ❏ Camera
- ❏ Starfish
- ❏ Bow brush

These three ponies were packaged with unnamed bonus baby ponies in some countries. Initially, it was unclear if these baby ponies would be sold within the United States. Many collectors had these sets imported so they could get the bonus baby ponies. Later, Target stores offered the white baby (Sandy Island) and the pink baby (Hula Lula) packaged as singles (see Target Exclusive Baby Ponies section). The yellow baby (Surf Star) was later offered in the US in an exclusive in the TRU Butterfly Island Adventure playset (see Butterfly Island Adventure in Building Playset section). However, the symbol of the Seaside Celebration bonus Surf Star is noticeably smaller than the symbol of TRU Butterfly Island Adventure Surf Star.

**Bumblesweet II packaged with bonus baby Hula Lula**

**Wysteria II packaged with bonus baby Surf Star**

*Cherry Blossom II and bonus baby Sandy Island is not pictured. Please see Target Exclusive Baby Ponies section for pictures.

# Seaside Celebration Ponies
### (second set)

This set of Seaside Celebration Ponies each came with a tropical friend.

❑ **Golden Delicious** (apple)
- ❑ Turtle Pal
- ❑ Sundress
- ❑ Surf board
- ❑ Frisbee
- ❑ Flower hair band
- ❑ Flower brush

❑ **Sew-and-So** (button and hearts)
- ❑ Monkey Pal
- ❑ Sarong
- ❑ Basket of bananas
- ❑ Tropical drink
- ❑ Flower hair band
- ❑ Flower brush

❏ **Skywishes** (kites)
    ❏ Parrot pal
    ❏ Grass skirt
    ❏ Flower lei
    ❏ Ukulele
    ❏ Drums
    ❏ Flower hair band
    ❏ Flower brush

# Shimmer Ponies

Shimmer Ponies have vividly colored bodies and glittery hair. Flippity Flop and Strawberry Reef were released shortly after the initial set of four Shimmer Ponies.

❑ **Fizzy Pop** (ice cream soda)
   ❑ Flower brush

❑ **Island Rainbow**
(island, palm tree, and a rainbow)
   ❑ Flower brush

❑ **Shell-belle** (coral and shells)
   ❑ Flower brush

❑ **Waterfire** (flame and waves)
   ❑ Flower brush

❑ **Flippity Flop** (flip flop sandals)
   ❑ Flower brush

❑ **Strawberry Reef** (coral and strawberry)
   ❑ Flower brush

# Spring/Easter Ponies

In 2005, more Spring themed ponies were released. In addition to a second set of Target exclusive Spring ponies, Pinkie Pie (III) and Butterscotch were dressed up in bunny costumes ready to celebrate. While these two ponies were initially difficult to find, they later were available on the KB toys website after the season had passed.

❏ **Lolligiggle (Target Exclusive)**(bunny)
- ❏ Bunny ears
- ❏ Bunny tail
- ❏ Bow brush

❏ **Skedoodle (Target Exclusive)**
(colored eggs)
- ❏ Bunny ears
- ❏ Tail ribbon
- ❏ Bow brush

❒ **Yesterdaisy (Target Exclusive)** (flower and sun)
  ❒ Pink checked hat
  ❒ Tail ribbon
  ❒ Bow brush

 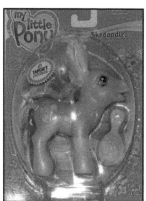 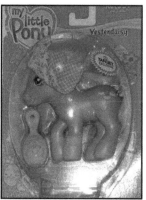

Pinkie Pie and Butterscotch came dressed in bunny ears and packaged in egg-shaped plastic packages.

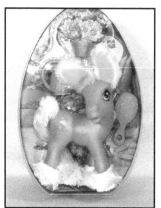 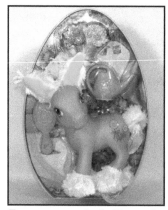

❒ **Pinkie Pie (III)** (balloons)          ❒ **Butterscotch** (lollipops)
  ❒ Bunny ears                              ❒ Bunny ears
  ❒ Cottontail                             ❒ Cottontail
  ❒ 4 bunny slippers                       ❒ 4 bunny slippers
  ❒ Watering can                           ❒ Watering can
  ❒ 2 bouquets                             ❒ 2 bouquets
  ❒ Flowerpot                              ❒ Flowerpot
  ❒ Hot Pink flower brush                  ❒ Hot Pink flower brush

# Sunny Scents Ponies
### (first set)

Sunny Scents ponies have scented bodies that smell like their symbol. For example, Coconut Grove smells like coconuts, Citrus Sweetheart smells like oranges, and Apple Spice smells like apples.

❑ **Apple Spice** (apple and flowers)
    ❑ Bow brush

❑ **Citrus Sweetheart** (oranges)
    ❑ Bow brush

❑ **Coconut Grove** (coconuts)
    ❑ Bow brush

❑ **Tropical Surprise** (tropical flowers)
    ❑ Bow brush

# Sunny Scents Ponies
**(second set)**

A second set of Sunny Scents Ponies was released in late 2005.

❏ **Lavender Lake** (flower and butterfly)
   ❏ Bow brush

❏ **Pineapple Paradise**
(pineapple and tropical drink)
   ❏ Bow brush

❏ **Tangerine Sunset** (tangerine and sunset)
   ❏ Bow brush

❏ **Thistle Whistle** (flowers)
   ❏ Bow brush

# Super Long-Hair Ponies

In 2005, four more Super-Long Hair Ponies were released. Dream Blue and Rainbowberry were released first and were not widely distributed within the U.S. During the summer months, Silver Lining and Dibble Dabble were also released.

❑ **Dream Blue** (wand, cloud, and moon)
- ❑ Crown
- ❑ Barrette
- ❑ Bow brush

❑ **Rainbowberry** (berries and rainbow)
- ❑ Crown
- ❑ Barrette
- ❑ Bow brush

❑ **Dibble Dabble**
(artist pallet and paint brush)
- ❑ Crown
- ❑ Barrette
- ❑ Flower brush

❑ **Silver Lining** (sun and clouds)
- ❑ Crown
- ❑ Barrette
- ❑ Flower brush

# Target Exclusive Baby Ponies

These baby ponies were packaged on a small card with a clothing accessory and a brush. They were released exclusively at Target stores and could usually be found at the check-out lane displays. They were released in sets of two. The first set was candy themed with Butterdrop and Penny Candy. The next set was beach themed with Hula Lula and Sandy Island. Hula Lula and Sandy Island had been released as part of bonus packs with Seaside Celebration ponies in other countries, but they did not have names until this release. Finally, two jewelry themed babies were added to the series: Charm Bracelet and Lavender Locket.

❐ **Butterdrop** (candy)
-   ❐ Hat
-   ❐ Bow brush

❐ **Penny Candy** (candy)
-   ❐ Hat
-   ❐ Bow brush

❐ **Hula Lula** (palm tree and island)
-   ❐ Visor
-   ❐ Bow brush

❐ **Sandy Island** (sand pail and shovel)
-   ❐ Visor
-   ❐ Bow brush

❑ **Charm Bracelet** (jewelry)
  ❑ Purple tutu
  ❑ Bow brush

❑ **Lavender Locket** (locket)
  ❑ White tutu
  ❑ Bow brush

# Valentine's Day Ponies

Target stores carried two exclusive Valentine's Day Ponies in 2005. Each pony came packaged on a bubble card with a heart-shaped bubble.

❏ **Always and Forever**
(Bow, arrow, and hearts)
- ❏ Crown
- ❏ Detachable wings
- ❏ Bow brush

❏ **Yours Truly**
(hearts)
- ❏ Crown
- ❏ Pants
- ❏ Bow brush

# Winter Baby Ponies

In December of 2005, two winter themed baby ponies were found at Meijer stores. They came packaged on small cards similar to the Target exclusive baby ponies. They had adorable winter hats and booties. While they do not have names printed on the boxes, a Meijer worker identified them by the names Jingle Jangle and Ribbons and Bows since those were the names associated with these ponies in their computer system. These ponies were fairly hard to find, but additional stock was found at discount chains in late 2006.

❑ **Jingle Jangle** (jingle bells)
    ❑ Winter hat
    ❑ 4 fuzzy booties
    ❑ Bow brush

❑ **Ribbons and Bows** (bows)
    ❑ Winter hat
    ❑ 4 fuzzy booties
    ❑ Bow brush

# Winter Ponies

In winter of 2005, a third set of three winter-themed ponies was released. Each pony had a winter themed cutie mark and was packaged in a box decorated with snowflakes with a brush and winter accessories. This set was sold exclusively at Target stores.

❑ **Minty** (mints)
    ❑ Scarf
    ❑ 4 winter socks
    ❑ Bow brush

❑ **Snow-Glo** (gift box)
    ❑ Winter hat
    ❑ Bow brush

❑ **Toboggan** (snowflake)
    ❑ Winter hat
    ❑ Bow brush

# Accessory Packs

Though not a part of the Butterfly Island set, 2005 also saw a new batch of ponies released with themed accessories. Many of these sets were store exclusive sets.

### Birthday Celebration with Sweetberry
- ❑ **Sweetberry (II)** (strawberries)
    - ❑ Birthday cake with candle
    - ❑ 2 slices of cake
    - ❑ 2 forks
    - ❑ Gift box
    - ❑ Pony party decoration
    - ❑ Birthday hat
    - ❑ Comb

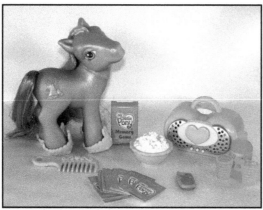

### Moonlight Celebration with Tink-a-Tink-a-Too
- ❑ **Tink-a-Tink-a-Too (II)** (bells)
    - ❑ Boom box
    - ❑ 4 bunny slippers
    - ❑ Bottle of soda
    - ❑ 2 cups
    - ❑ Bowl of popcorn
    - ❑ Cell phone
    - ❑ Pony match game with cards
    - ❑ Comb

Ponyville Picnic with Rainbow Dash
☐ **Rainbow Dash (IV)** (rainbow and clouds)
    ☐ Boom box
    ☐ Picnic basket
    ☐ Visor
    ☐ Bottle of soda
    ☐ 2 glasses
    ☐ 2 sandwiches
    ☐ Cell phone
    ☐ Comb

Petal Blossom Accessory Set
☐ **Petal Blossom** (flowers)
    ☐ Picnic basket
    ☐ 3 sets of 2 apples
    ☐ Barrette
    ☐ Brush with apple decal

### Seaside Surprise with Sweet Summertime
- ☐ **Sweet Summertime** (beach ball)
  - ☐ Sandcastle with crab friend
  - ☐ Surf Board
  - ☐ Beach tote
  - ☐ Water bottle
  - ☐ Sun shaped sunglasses
  - ☐ Frisbee
  - ☐ 3 shells
  - ☐ Towel
  - ☐ Mirrored brush

This set was exclusive to Toys R Us stores and was sold in a beach ball shaped bag.

### Summer Shores and Ocean Dreamer Set
- ☐ **Summer Shores** (3 fish and swirls)
- ☐ **Ocean Dreamer** (fish and swirls)
  - ☐ Pink Adult swimsuit
  - ☐ Pink adult hat
  - ☐ Orange and yellow baby hat
  - ☐ Boom box
  - ☐ Sandcastle
  - ☐ Camera
  - ☐ Pail
  - ☐ Glasses
  - ☐ Bow brush

This set was available exclusively at Target stores and came packaged in a clear plastic tote bag.

Close-up symbol pictures of Summer Shores and Ocean Dreamer

### Royalette Set
- ❏ **Royalette** (crown)
    - ❏ Vanity
    - ❏ Skirt
    - ❏ Crown
    - ❏ Barrette
    - ❏ Bow brush

This set was available exclusively at Target stores.

Close up of Royalette's symbol

### Fancy Flora and Sunshine Blossom
- ❏ **Fancy Flora** (flowers)
- ❏ **Sunshine Blossom** (flowers)
    - ❏ Hat
    - ❏ Skirt
    - ❏ Fruit stand
    - ❏ 2 baskets of berries
    - ❏ 2 trays of fruit
    - ❏ Bananas
    - ❏ Watering can
    - ❏ 2 bunches of flowers
    - ❏ 2 vases
    - ❏ 2 barrettes
    - ❏ Flower brush

A picture of this item was first seen online in the fall of 2004, but it wasn't available until the fall of 2005 when it was spotted in Canada and the UK. It was later available at K-mart stores.

## Beach Belle and Caribbean Delight

Beach Belle and Caribbean Delight without their outfits.

- ❏ **Beach Belle** (flowers)
- ❏ **Caribbean Delight** (parrot)
  - ❏ Sundress
  - ❏ Hat
  - ❏ Skirt
  - ❏ Flower brush
  - ❏ Flower brush

This set was sold exclusively at Menard's stores during the 2005 holiday season. Both of these ponies are Super Long-Hair ponies.

# Spring Basket

The Spring Basket contained three ponies and multiple accessories packaged in a bucket made to look like a basket. The accessories included in this set came in a variety of colors.

❏ **Dainty Daisy** (daisies in a basket)

❏ **Lullabelle** (bells and ribbon)

❏ **Spring Breeze** (kite, clouds, and sun)

**Spring Basket Accessories**
❏ Table with "growing" daisies
❏ Table
❏ Picnic basket
❏ 3 slices of cake
❏ 3 teacups
❏ 3 saucers
❏ 3 forks
❏ 3 pink charms
❏ Charm bracelets
❏ Heart brush

# Special Ponies and Packs

Several ponies were released in 2005 that did not belong to any certain set. This section is designated to feature these ponies.

## Pony Project

This pony was available at the San Diego Comic Con at a booth that promoted The Pony Project, an art exhibit in New York City. A unique feature of this pony is that it has The Pony Project logo stamped on both sides.

❏ **San Diego Pony Project White Pony**
    ❏ Bow brush

This pony was available at The Pony Project art exhibit in New York City. A unique feature of this pony is that it has The Pony Project logo stamped on both sides.

❏ **NYC Pony Project Black Pony**
    ❏ Bow brush

## My Little Pony Fair

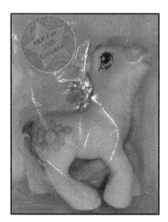
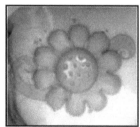

Hasbro donated 300 Bay Breeze ponies to be given out to attendees of the 2005 My Little Pony Fair in Minneapolis, Minnesota. Recipients were required to sign a contract, which stated they would not sell her for monetary gain on any online sites.

❏ **Bay Breeze** (flower and wave design)

## Musical Wishes Jewelry Box
- ❏ **Skywishes** (kite and butterfly)
  - ❏ Jewelry box
  - ❏ 2 rings
  - ❏ Charm bracelet
  - ❏ Pony charm necklace
  - ❏ 2 barrettes
  - ❏ Bow brush

Mint in box picture of Magical Wishes Jewelry box

A later release of this set contained a bonus baby Flower Flash in its packaging.

When you turn the platform on the jewelry box, it plays music.

Mint in box picture of Hidden Treasure

## Hidden Treasure
- ❏ **Hidden Treasure** (jeweled star)
  - ❏ *Friends are Never Far Away* DVD
  - ❏ Treasure chest
  - ❏ Crown
  - ❏ Beaded necklace
  - ❏ Ring
  - ❏ Butterfly barrette
  - ❏ Flower hair band
  - ❏ Flower brush

# Avon Catalogue Sets

**Avon Catalogue Exclusive Peach Surprise and Baby Tea Lily**
- ❑ **Peach Surprise** (Peach)
- ❑ **Baby Tea Lily** (lily)
    - ❑ 2 sticker sheets
    - ❑ Bow brush

**Avon Catalogue Exclusive Jazz Matazz and Baby Wave Catcher**
- ❑ **Jazz Matazz** (trumpet)
- ❑ **Baby Wave Catcher** (sun and wave)
    - ❑ 2 sticker sheets
    - ❑ Bow brush

My Little Pony Playhouse: Book and Beauty Set was offered exclusively through Avon catalogues. It contained a Sunny Daze figure with a molded tail, a comb, and books.

# Toys R Us 4-Pack

This 4-Pack was available exclusively at Toys R Us stores. It included four ponies:
Cotton Candy (in a new pose), Rainbow Swirl (reissue), Candy Apple, and Finger Paints.
This set was available in time for the 2005 holiday season.

❒ **Cotton Candy** (cotton candy)
   ❒ Flower brush

❒ **Finger Paints**
(artist pallet and paint brush)
   ❒ Flower brush

❒ **Candy Apple** (candy apples)
   ❒ Flower brush

❒ **Rainbow Swirl** (glitter sundae)
   ❒ Flower brush

Mint in box picture of Toys R Us 4-Pack

93

# KB Toys Exclusive

☐ **Kimono II** (lanterns)
☐ bow brush

Kimono II was available on a single pack card exclusively at KB Toy stores

# Rosey Posey

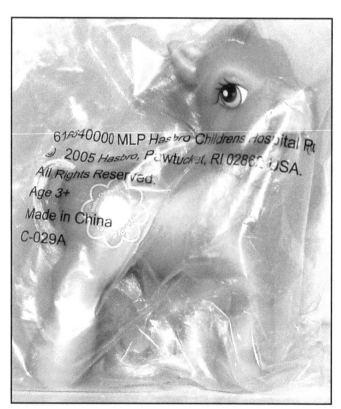

☐ **Rosey Posey**
(two dolphins inside a flower with the words, "Hasbro Children's Hospital Caring for Kids")

Rosey Posey was given out exclusively to attendees of the 2005 Hasbro Children's Hospital charity ball.

*Picture of Rosey Posey provided by Diana Aselage

# 2006
## Crystal Princess

# Balloon Flying Ponies

Cherry Blossom, Merriweather, and Sweet Breeze were all re-released in new poses with hot air balloons. Bonus Breezie ponies were included in many packages. Sweet Breeze was packaged with bonus Breezies in Canada. Special bracelets were also available in some packages to hold bonus jewels that were packaged with some Crystal Princess ponies. Cherry Blossom was also available without a Breezie packaged with a watering can, 2 flowers, and a planter.

**Balloon Flying with Cherry Blossom**
- ❏ **Cherry Blossom III** (flowers)
- ❏ **Tiddly Wink** (daisy)
  - ❏ Hot air balloon
  - ❏ Bow brush

**Balloon Flying with Merriweather**
- ❏ **Merriweather II** (glitter umbrella)
- ❏ **Tra-La-La** (pink flower)
  - ❏ Hot air balloon
  - ❏ Bow Brush

- ❏ **Tiddly Wink**
(bonus Breezie packaged with Cherry Blossom)

- ❏ **Tra-La-La**
(bonus Breezie packaged with Merriweather)

**Balloon Flying with Sweet Breeze**
☐ **Sweet Breeze II** (cloud and flowers)
☐ **Daylily** (tulip)
    ☐ Hot air balloon
    ☐ Bow brush

☐ **Daylily**
(bonus Breezie packaged with Sweet Breeze)

☐ **Willow Whisp** (pink and white flower)
☐ **Knick-Knack** (pink flower with green stem)

# Birthflower Birthday Ponies

Birthflower Ponies were sold exclusively at Toys R Us stores. There are twelve ponies in this set (one pony for each month of the year). Birthflower Ponies have a flower symbol that matches the pony's month.

❒ **January Carnation** (carnation)
  ❒ Bow brush

❒ **February Violet** (violet)
  ❒ Bow brush

❒ **March Daffodil** (daffodil)
  ❒ Bow brush

❒ **April Daisy** (daisy)
  ❒ Bow brush

❒ **May Lily of the Valley** (Lily of the Valley)
  ❒ Bow brush

❒ **June Rose** (rose)
  ❒ Bow brush

❏ **July Larkspur** (larkspur)
    ❏ Bow brush

❏ **August Gladiolas** (gladiolas)
    ❏ Bow brush

❏ **September Aster** (aster)
    ❏ Bow brush

❏ **October Calendula** (calendula)
    ❏ Bow brush

❏ **November Chrysanthemum**
(chrysanthemum)
    ❏ Bow brush

❏ **December Poinsettia** (poinsettia)
    ❏ Bow brush

# Breezies Parade

The first two sets of Breezies Parade Ponies had colored petal cars that matched the Breezies' tiaras. These Petal cars could be attached to the Carriage Ponies' carriages.

- ❏ **Tumbletop** (flowers and swirls)
- ❏ **Fluffaluff** (tulip and dots)
- ❏ **Silly Lilly** (lily)
    - ❏ 3 petal cars
    - ❏ 3 tiaras
    - ❏ Comb

- ❏ **Azalea Bloom** (azalea blossom)
- ❏ **Meadow Moon** (moon over a meadow)
- ❏ **Honeydew Hum** (purple flower, blue leaves)
    - ❏ 3 petal cars
    - ❏ 3 tiaras
    - ❏ Comb

# Carriage Ponies

Carriage Ponies were sold with carriages that could attach to the Breezie petal cars. The birds located on the front of the carriage are detachable. In Australia, an additional set, Holiday Hooray with Snow-Glo was released. Snow-Glo was previously available as a Target exclusive during the holiday season of 2005.

☐ **Pretty Parasol** (glittery parasol)
- ☐ Carriage with 2 detachable birds
- ☐ Crown
- ☐ Bow brush

☐ **Cute Curtsey** (bow and flowers)
- ☐ Carriage with 2 detachable birds
- ☐ Crown
- ☐ Bow brush

☐ **Holiday Hooray with Snow-Glo\***
(gift box)
- ☐ Carriage with 2 detachable birds
- ☐ Winter hat
- ☐ Bow brush

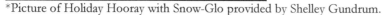

\*Picture of Holiday Hooray with Snow-Glo provided by Shelley Gundrum.

# Crystal Design Ponies

Crystal Design Ponies have raised three dimensional symbols with the exception of Star Flower.

❏ **Wind Drifter** (butterfly)
　❏ Bow brush

❏ **Royal Bouquet** (flower)
　❏ Bow brush

❏ **Lovey Dovey** (heart)
　❏ Bow brush

❏ **Sunny Sparkle** (flower)
　❏ Bow brush

❏ **Star Surprise** (star)
　❏ Bow brush

❏ **Daybreak** (butterfly)
　❏ Bow brush

❐ **Peach Blossom** (3D flower)
    ❐ Bow brush

❐ **Star Flower** (tropical flower)
    ❐ Bow brush

❐ **Love-A-Belle** (3D hearts)
    ❐ Bow brush

❐ **Rhapsody Ribbons**
(3D flower with ribbon and hearts)
    ❐ Bow brush

# Cutie Cascade Ponies

Cutie Cascade Ponies have symbols that cascade down their back leg. The first group of Cutie Cascade Ponies released in the Crystal Princess line, have glittery markings while some later released groups have raised designs, glittery symbols and gradient coloring on their legs.

❏ **Fairy Dust** (glittery butterfly)
  ❏ Bow brush

❏ **Tulip Twinkle** (glittery tulips)
  ❏ Bow brush

❏ **Amazing Grace** (diamonds and swirls)
  ❏ Bow brush

❏ **Sweet Sparkle** (lollipop and ribbons)
  ❏ Bow brush

❏ **Jade Garden** (flower bouquet)
  ❏ Bow brush

❏ **Blushie** (raised flowers and ribbons)
  ❏ Bow brush

❏ **Twilight Pink**
(heart with wings and ribbon)
 ❏ Bow brush

❏ **Silver Rain** (bow, ribbons and flowers)
 ❏ Bow brush

❏ **Comet Tail** (stars and ribbons)
 ❏ Bow brush

❏ **Morning Glory**
(bird, branch, rainbow and music notes)
 ❏ Bow brush

❏ **Swirlypop** (lollipop and hearts)
 ❏ Bow brush

❏ **Dream Drifter**
(tie-dyed design with heart)
 ❏ Bow brush

# Deluxe Pegasus Ponies

Deluxe Pegasus ponies have unique wings that go up and down by pressing their cutie mark. In some parts of Europe, these two Deluxe Pegasus Ponies were packaged with a bonus Breezie. Star Flight was packaged with Knick-Knack and Heart Bright was packaged with Willow Whisp. Both of these bonus Breezies were available in the Balloon Flying with Sweet Breeze set that was available for a short time in Canada.

❒ **Star Flight**
(star with small trailing stars and dots)
  - ❒ Crown
  - ❒ 2 star barrettes
  - ❒ Rose brush

❒ **Heart Bright**
(heart with trailing hearts and dots)
  - ❒ Crown
  - ❒ 2 heart barrettes
  - ❒ Rose brush

❒ **Willow Whisp**
  (pink and white flower)
❒ **Knick-Knack**
  (pink flower with green stem)

# Discount Ponies

This set of ponies was available at discount chains throughout the US including Family Dollar stores, Big Lots stores and Value City stores. Some collectors may refer to them as "Family Dollar Ponies" since that is where they were initially discovered. These four adult ponies are sold on small cards. Each pony came packaged with a brush.

❏ **Sunrise** (rising sun)
    ❏ Bow brush

❏ **Chocolate Delight**
(hearts and chocolate cake)
    ❏ Bow brush

❏ **Green Apple** (green apple)
    ❏ Bow brush

❏ **Rhythm and Rhyme**
(heart music notes and circles)
    ❏ Bow brush

# Divine Shine

Reminiscent of G1 Sparkle Ponies, these G3 Ponies have glittery plastic and tinseled hair.

❏ **Secret Wish** (star wand)
    ❏ Bow brush

❏ **Glitterbelle** (ring)
    ❏ Bow brush

❏ **Tangerine Twinkle** (heart)
    ❏ Bow brush

❏ **Flower Garland** (daisy chain)
    ❏ Bow brush

# Fancy Hair Ponies

In 2006, the Super-Long Hair Ponies were replaced with Fancy Hair Ponies. Precious Gem was packaged with a Breezie, Rose Garden, in Europe. Petite Petunia was sold in Europe and was not available in the United States or Canada. Two other ponies, Rainbow Treat and Royal Beauty, were available in parts of Europe but not sold in North America.

❒ **Precious Gem**
(light blue jewel with diamond, flower, and swirl design)
    ❒ Purple heart hand mirror
    ❒ Purple butterfly clip with yellow hair
    ❒ Purple hair pick

❒ **Petite Petunia**
(pink jewel with flower and dot design)
    ❒ Purple heart hand mirror
    ❒ Purple butterfly clip with purple hair
    ❒ Pink hair pick

❒ **Rainbow Treat**
(ice cream cone and hearts)
    ❒ Pink heart hand mirror
    ❒ White butterfly clip with ribbons
    ❒ Bow brush

❒ **Royal Beauty** (flower bouquets)
    ❒ Purple/pink heart hand mirror
    ❒ Purple/pink butterfly clip with ribbons
    ❒ Bow brush

□ **Rose Garden (European bonus Breezie)** (3 flowers)

# Fun with Ponies

These sets were sold at discount stores within the US. They contain re-released ponies and accessories.

❐ **Bunches-O-Fun** (bouquet of flowers)
- ❐ Pink boa
- ❐ 2 hangers
- ❐ Skirt
- ❐ Blue barrette
- ❐ Bow brush

❐ **Gardenia Glow** (gardenia flowers)
- ❐ Polka dot hat
- ❐ Beach bag
- ❐ Water bottle
- ❐ Lunch box
- ❐ Strawberries
- ❐ Camera
- ❐ Bow brush

❐ **Sparkleworks II** (fireworks)
- ❐ Skirt
- ❐ 4 white shoes
- ❐ Radio
- ❐ Small bottle
- ❐ Barrette
- ❐ Bow brush

# Halloween Ponies

In the fall of 2006, a set of two Halloween-themed ponies was released. Each pony had a Halloween themed cutie mark and was packaged on a card that was shaped like a pumpkin with a Halloween costume and a brush. This set was sold exclusively at Target stores.

❏ **Abra-ca-dabra** (candy corn)
   - ❏ Witch hat
   - ❏ Black cape
   - ❏ Bow brush

❏ **Pumpkin Tart** (cat and moon)
   - ❏ Cat ears
   - ❏ Black ribbon
   - ❏ Bow brush

# Pegasus Ponies

The Crystal Princess line included many new and exciting Pegasus Ponies. These Pegasus Ponies have painted wing tips with a pearly sheen. Some wings are also lightly dusted with glitter. Both Windy Wisp and Aurora Mist have glittery jewels as their symbols.

❑ **Royal Rose** (roses)
  ❑ Bow brush

❑ **Silver Glow** (stars)
  ❑ Bow brush

❑ **Morning Monarch** (butterfly)
  ❑ Bow brush

❑ **Twirlerina** (flowers)
  ❑ Bow brush

❑ **Daisy May** (daisies)
  ❑ Bow brush

❑ **Twinkle Bloom** (flowers)
  ❑ Bow brush

117

❑ **Windy Wisp** (jeweled flower and flowers)
   ❑ Bow brush

❑ **Pearly Pie** (flowers)
   ❑ Bow brush

❑ **Aurora Mist** (jeweled starfish and shell)
   ❑ Bow brush

# Ponies on the Go

Two more ponies were released during the Crystal Princess line sporting scooters. Both Cupcake and Lullabelle had been previously released in different poses. These ponies were widely available at most retailers. The satchel and camera accessory pieces were available in alternate colors.

❏ **Cupcake II** (cupcakes)
    ❏ Scooter
    ❏ Helmet
    ❏ Flag
    ❏ Satchel*
    ❏ Camera*
    ❏ Bow brush

❏ **Lullabelle II** (bells and ribbon)
    ❏ Scooter
    ❏ Helmet
    ❏ Flag
    ❏ Satchel*
    ❏ Camera*
    ❏ Bow brush

*This pony was also sold with a yellow satchel and purple camera

*This pony was also sold with a yellow satchel and aqua camera

# Pony and Me/ Let's Go

These sets contained a pony and purse. In Europe, Fluttershy was packaged with a bonus Breezie, Lady Slipper.

☐ **Fluttershy III** (butterfly)
- ☐ Purse
- ☐ Crown
- ☐ Bow brush

☐ **Lady Slipper**
**(European bonus Breezie)**
(pink flower with purple leaves)

☐ **Twinkle Twirl II** (stars and swirl)
- ☐ Purse
- ☐ Crown
- ☐ Bow brush

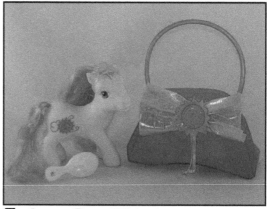

☐ **Sunny Daze IV** (sun)
- ☐ Purse
- ☐ Crown
- ☐ Bow brush

# Pretty Patterns Ponies

Pretty Patterns Ponies have gradient coloring on their legs. Most also have multiple markings along the bottom portion of their bodies. All but Daisy Paisley have tinsel in their hair.

☐ **Fancy Free** (hearts)
   ☐ Bow brush

☐ **Summer Bloom** (flowers)
   ☐ Bow brush

☐ **Royal Twist** (flowers and swirls)
   ☐ Bow brush

☐ **Midnight Dreams** (moon and stars)
   ☐ Bow brush

☐ **Daisy Paisley** (paisley design)
☐ Bow brush

# Sister Sets

Sister sets included an adult pony and a smaller pony. The smaller pony is significantly larger than the previously released baby ponies. Both ponies share similar cutie marks and were packaged with themed accessories.

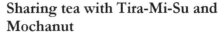

**Ballet with Dance Slippers and Dance Around**

- ❐ **Dance Slippers** (ballet slipper)
- ❐ **Dance Around** (2 ballet slippers)
    - ❐ Mirror
    - ❐ Boom box
    - ❐ 2 crowns
    - ❐ 2 tutus
    - ❐ 2 sets of 4 ballet slippers
    - ❐ 2 bouquets
    - ❐ 2 purses
    - ❐ Bow brush

**Sharing tea with Tira-Mi-Su and Mochanut**

- ❐ **Tira-Mi-Su** (teacup)
- ❐ **Mochanut** (2 teacups)
    - ❐ Table
    - ❐ Serving Tray
    - ❐ 2 crowns
    - ❐ 2 skirts
    - ❐ 2 sets of shoes
    - ❐ 2 cookie plates
    - ❐ 2 tea cups
    - ❐ Teapot and sugar bowl
    - ❐ 2 spoons
    - ❐ Bow brush

Close up symbol pictures of Dance Slippers and Dance Around.

Close up symbol pictures of Tira-Mi-Su and Mochanut

# Spring/ Easter Ponies
### (Target Exclusive)

In 2006, more Easter themed ponies were released. In addition to a third set of Target exclusive Easter ponies, Daisyjo was sold in an egg-shaped plastic package dressed in a bunny costume.

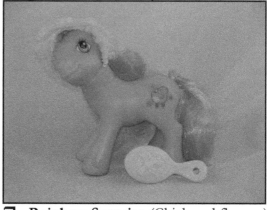

❏ **Gigglebean** (Easter eggs and a chocolate bunny)
- ❏ Cloth hat
- ❏ Bow brush

❏ **Rainbow Surprise** (Chick and flowers)
- ❏ Lace hat
- ❏ Bow brush

❏ **Sunshine Parade** (Easter basket with eggs)
- ❏ Bunny ears
- ❏ Bunny tail
- ❏ Bow Brush

❏ **Daisyjo** (daisies)
- ❏ Bunny Ears
- ❏ Cottontail
- ❏ 4 bunny slippers
- ❏ Watering Can
- ❏ 2 bouquets
- ❏ Flowerpot
- ❏ Bow brush

In 2007, three more Easter themed ponies were released. These ponies were available at many different retail stores.

□ **Bashful Bonnet** (bonnet with flowers)
   □ Pink cloth hat

□ **Flower Wishes**
(watering can, shovel, and flower)
   □ Bunny ears

□ **Morning Dawn Delight** (egg with chick)
   □ Wings

# Styling Ponies

Styling ponies were very large My Little ponies that had long manes and tails that could be styled using included accessories. Later releases of these ponies contained extra bonus accessories.

☐ **Styling Pinkie Pie**

☐ **Styling Rainbow Dash**

☐ **Styling Rarity**

☐ **Styling Cheerilee**

# Target Exclusive Baby Ponies

These baby ponies were packaged on a small card with a brush. They were released at Target stores and could usually be found at check-out lane displays. They were released in sets of two. Hokey Pokey and Boogie Woogie made up the first set and Northern Lights and Winter Ice made up the Winter Baby set. In 2007, both Boogie Woogie and Hokey Pokey were found at K-Mart stores with movable heads, slightly shorter legs and more rounded ears.

❒ **Hokey Pokey**

(flowers)

❒ Sticker sheet

❒ Bow brush

❒ **Boogie Woogie**

(keyboard and music notes)

❒ Sticker sheet

❒ Bow brush

❒ **Northern Lights**

(snowflake and rainbow)

❒ Scarf

❒ Bow brush

❒ **Winter Ice**

(snow man and snow flakes)

❒ Scarf

❒ Bow brush

# Unicorn Ponies

The Crystal Princess line featured the first unicorns of this generation.

❏ **Whistle Wishes** (stars and cloud)
  ❏ Bow brush

❏ **Brights Brightly** (rising sun and hearts)
  ❏ Bow brush

❏ **Sunrise Song** (tropical bird)
  ❏ Bow brush

❏ **Garden Wishes** (glitter flower)
  ❏ Bow brush

# Valentine's Day Ponies

In 2006, Hasbro released two Valentine's Day Ponies, Wish-I-May and Wish-I-Might, exclusively at Target stores. All My Heart and Candy Heart, another set of two Valentine's Day Ponies, were released in 2007. The 2007 Valentine Ponies were not exclusive to Target stores and could be found at multiple retail stores.

❏ **Wish-I-May** (heart balloons)
- ❏ Wings
- ❏ Heart pendant
- ❏ Bow bush

❏ **Wish-I-Might** (box of chocolates)
- ❏ Skirt
- ❏ Purse
- ❏ Bow brush

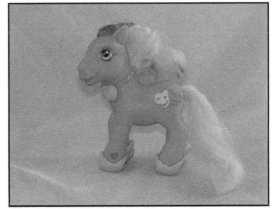

❏ **All My Heart** (heart lollipops)
- ❏ Heart antenna headband
- ❏ 4 red shoes

❏ **Candy Heart** (smiling hearts)
- ❏ Necklace
- ❏ 4 pink shoes

# Winter Ponies

In winter of 2006, a fourth set of three winter-themed ponies was released. Each pony had a winter themed "cutie mark" and was packaged in a box decorated with snowflakes with a brush and winter accessories. This set was sold exclusively at Target stores.

❏ **Velvet Bow** (star)
- ❏ Winter hat
- ❏ Scarf
- ❏ Bow brush

❏ **Winter Wish** (sleigh and bells)
- ❏ Reindeer antlers
- ❏ Jingle bell collar
- ❏ Bow brush

❏ **Chilly Breezes** (skis and ski poles)
- ❏ Winter hat
- ❏ Ski mask
- ❏ Bow brush

# Accessory Packs

During the Crystal Princess line, many new accessory packs were released. These sets consisted of a pony or ponies and various themed accessories.

## Crystal Princess Bride
- ☐ **Wysteria III** (flowers)
  - ☐ Wedding arch
  - ☐ Wedding cake
  - ☐ Wedding dress
  - ☐ Veil and crown
  - ☐ Bouquet
  - ☐ Bracelet
  - ☐ 4 shoes
  - ☐ Comb

## Crystal Slipper Princess
- ☐ **Desert Rose** (glitter rose)
  - ☐ Mirrored vanity
  - ☐ Dress
  - ☐ Necklace
  - ☐ Crown
  - ☐ Earrings
  - ☐ Heart barrette
  - ☐ 4 shoes
  - ☐ Comb

Both Shimmer Shine and Graceful Glimmer had special light-up features that could be activated by pressing a flower button located on their head. Graceful Glimmer's tiara lights up while Shimmer Shine's rump glows.

Flower Petal Princess
☐ **Shimmer Shine** (flower)
    ☐ Lace dress
    ☐ Necklace
    ☐ Barrette
    ☐ Rose brush

Winter Crystal Princess
☐ **Graceful Glimmer** (bouquet of flowers)
    ☐ Veil and crown
    ☐ Dress
    ☐ Bracelet
    ☐ Barrette
    ☐ Rose brush

These sets were available at discount chains such as Big Lots and Family Dollar stores. Jazz Matazz, Wave Catcher, Tea Lily, and Peach Surprise (formerly Avon catalogue exclusives) were packaged in these sets along with matte versions of Magic Marigold and Sweetberry.

**My Little Pony Popcorn Fun**
- ❏ **Jazz Matazz** (trumpet)
- ❏ **Wave Catcher** (sun and wave)
- ❏ **Magic Marigold**
(top hat, marigolds, and cane)

- ❏ Popcorn stand
- ❏ 2 bags of popcorn
- ❏ Bow brush

**Sleepover Dreams**
- ❏ **Tea Lily** (lily)
- ❏ **Sweetberry** (strawberries)
- ❏ **Peach Surprise** (peach)

- ❏ Bed
- ❏ 4 slippers
- ❏ Sleep mask
- ❏ Bow brush

# Spring Basket

The Spring Basket contained three ponies and multiple accessories packaged in a bucket made to look like a basket. The accessories included in this set came in a variety of colors.

❒ **Lavender Cloud** (cloud and flowers)
    ❒ Flower brush

❒ **Berries 'n Cherries**
(raspberry, cherry, and flowers)
    ❒ Flower brush

❒ **Spring Carnivale** (3 flowers)
    ❒ Flower brush

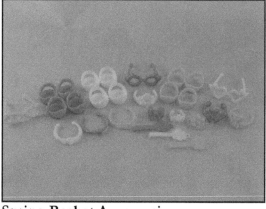

**Spring Basket Accessories**
    ❒ 3 pairs of glasses
    ❒ 3 pairs of shoes
    ❒ 3 necklaces
    ❒ 3 tiaras
    ❒ 3 bracelets
    ❒ 3 barrettes

# Special Ponies and Packs

Several ponies were released during 2006 that did not belong to any certain set. This section is designated to feature these ponies.

### Dream Blue II
❑ **Dream Blue**
(wand, cloud, and moon)
      ❑ Bow brush

This version of Dream Blue was available exclusively at KB toy stores.

### Rarity the Unicorn
❑ **Rarity**
(glittery heart and rainbow)
      ❑ *Music video DVD*
      ❑ Treasure chest
      ❑ Magic wand
      ❑ Pearl necklace
      ❑ Bow barrette with ribbon
      ❑ 3 barrettes
      ❑ Bow brush

Rarity was the first Unicorn pony available in the G3 line.

## Grand Puzzleventure
☐ **Puzzlement**
(magnifying glass and puzzle piece)
    ☐ TV plug-in game
    ☐ Bow brush

This set included a joystick that could be plugged into a television set to allow you to play a series of games.

## Lily Lightly
☐ **Lily Lightly** (lily)
    ☐ Attached dress and necklace
    ☐ 4 white shoes
    ☐ 2 hair barrettes
    ☐ Star wand brush

Lily Lightly's eyes blink and her dress lights up when the star on her chest is pressed. The dress and necklace are attached to the pony and are not removable.

Close up of Lily Lightly's symbol

Licensing Show Rarity
❏ **Rarity**
(glittery heart and rainbow with the words
"Licensing Show Hasbro 2006")*
❏ Brush

This version of Rarity had short hair and
was given out to attendees of the 2006
Licensing Show.

*Picture of Licensing Show Rarity provided by
Linda Murphy

JC Penny Set
❏ **Tea Lily** (lily)
❏ **Jazz Matazz** (trumpet)
❏ **Peach Surprise** (peach)
❏ **Wave Catcher** (sun and wave)
    ❏ Watering trough (Grand Champions)
    ❏ Box (Grand Champions)
    ❏ 4 sticker sheets
    ❏ 5 ribbon/strings
    ❏ 3 jeweled bands
    ❏ 3 flower bands
    ❏ 3 star picks
    ❏ 3 bow barrettes
    ❏ 2 bow brushes

This set consisted of the four ponies that
were previously exclusive to Avon. It was
available through the JC Penny online
store. Both the water trough and the box
are marked "Grand Champions." This is
interesting because the Grand Champion
line is produced by Mattel and not
Hasbro.

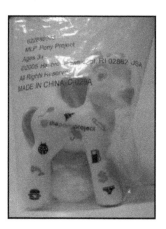

❏ **Twice-As-Fancy Project Pony**
(various designs from the pony project artwork)*

    ❏ Bow brush

This pony was available in limited quantities and was produced to commemorate NYC Pony Project.

*Picture of TAF Project Pony provided by Karen P. Wills

**Sharing Tea with Pinkie Pie and Minty**
❏ **Pinkie Pie IV** (balloons)
❏ **Minty IV** (mints)

This set was only available at the My Little Pony Live Show.

# MLP Fair Ponies

While these ponies were not officially produced by Hasbro, I feel that they deserve to be included. Frisco and Trolley were created using Love Wishes ponies that were donated to the MLP Fair staff. The symbol was designed by the MLP Fair staff and then engraved into the pony's body. These ponies were limited to 150 pieces each and were packaged with a numbered card. The ponies were then sold online as well as at the My Little Pony Fair Convention in San Francisco.

**Frisco's symbol depicts the Golden Gate Bridge**

❏ **Frisco**
    ❏ Numbered Card

**Trolley's symbol is a San Francisco Trolley.**

❏ **Trolley**
    ❏ Numbered Card

# Building Playsets

# Celebration Castle

Celebration Castle was released in 2003 along with the initial wave of G3 ponies. It is with this playset that the first baby G3 pony, Pink Sunsparkle, was offered. This playset was widely available at most major retailers. In 2004, this playset was reissued with a bonus baby pony, Baby Romperooni, and sold exclusively at Toys R Us stores. Baby Romperooni had initially been packaged with Super Long-Hair Rainbow Flash in 2003, but she did not yet have a name at that time.

☐ **Pink Sunsparkle**
(shining heart inside a heart)
- ☐ Stove that opens to a sink
- ☐ Elevator
- ☐ Toy chest
- ☐ Bed
- ☐ Vanity
- ☐ Wardrobe
- ☐ Dresser
- ☐ Hanger
- ☐ Charm with ribbon
- ☐ Removable spinning disk
- ☐ Crown
- ☐ Teapot
- ☐ 2 teacups
- ☐ 2 saucers
- ☐ 2 forks
- ☐ Sauce pan
- ☐ Bow brush
- ☐ Comb
- ☐ Tutu

This hot air balloon was also included in the Celebration Castle playset.

Baby Pink Sunsparkle was sold with the Celebration Castle, but also was later released in a Target Exclusive 3 Pack in 2004.

Celebration Castle plays music and lights up.

The packaging changed from the large window packaging (shown at right) to packaging with a much smaller window after the initial run.

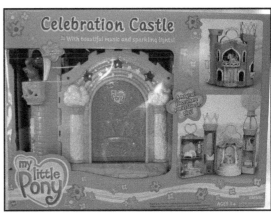

# Cotton Candy Café

- ❑ **Cotton Candy** (cotton candy)
    - ❑ Cash register
    - ❑ Oven
    - ❑ Table
    - ❑ 2 teacups
    - ❑ 2 saucers
    - ❑ 2 pieces of cake
    - ❑ Carded punch-out food
    - ❑ Heart brush with decal
    - ❑ Charm

**Exterior view of Cotton Candy Cafe**

**Mint in Box Cotton Candy Cafe**

# Bloomin' Blossoms Shop
## (Wal-Mart exclusive)

☐ **Meadowbrook** (dragonfly and flower)

- ☐ Popcorn stand
- ☐ 2 boxes of popcorn
- ☐ Cash register with conveyor
- ☐ Fruit stand
- ☐ 2 baskets of berries
- ☐ 2 fruit trays
- ☐ Bananas
- ☐ Potted topiary
- ☐ Watering can
- ☐ Flower storage container
- ☐ Table with "growing" flower
- ☐ 3 reversible flowers
- ☐ 2 vases
- ☐ Milk carton
- ☐ Small bottle
- ☐ 2 small can goods
- ☐ Round canister
- ☐ Cereal box
- ☐ 6 cans (molded together)
- ☐ Bow brush

**Exterior view of Bloomin' Blossoms Shop**

**Mint in Box Bloomin' Blossoms Shop**

# Celebration Salon

☐ **Amberlocks**
(bows, locks of hair, and purple circle)

- ☐ Cash register
- ☐ Sink/vanity combo
- ☐ Standing mirror
- ☐ Hanger
- ☐ Tutu

- ☐ 2 small bottles
- ☐ 2 barrettes
- ☐ Hair band
- ☐ Charm and ribbon
- ☐ Flower brush
- ☐ Comb

**Exterior view of Celebration Salon**

**Mint in Box Celebration Salon Value Pack**
Celebration Salon was sold packaged alone
and also in a Value Pack with Minty, Autumn
Skye, and Meadowbrook.

# Sweet Reflections Dress Shop

This set was available exclusively at Sam's Club stores in the US. It came with two new ponies (Darling Dahlia, and Goodie Goodie) and two reissued ponies (Skywishes and Periwinkle). This playset was made using the Cotton Candy Café mold, but had different coloring. This set was difficult for many collectors to find as it was part of a limited run. However, in 2005, the Sweet reflections Dress shop would be found at Argos stores in the UK.

- ❐ **Darling Dahlia** (flower bouquet)
- ❐ **Goodie Goodie** (hand mirror)
- ❐ **Skywishes** (kites)
- ❐ **Periwinkle** (jeweled design)
    - ❐ Cash register
    - ❐ Sink/vanity combo
    - ❐ Floral skirt
    - ❐ Shiny skirt
    - ❐ Purple dress
    - ❐ Green dotted cape
    - ❐ Hanger
    - ❐ 2 small bottles
    - ❐ 2 barrettes
    - ❐ Flower brush
    - ❐ Comb

❑ **Darling Dahlia**
(flower bouquet)

❑ **Goodie Goodie**
(hand mirror)

**Exterior view of Sweet Reflections Dress Shop**

**Mint in Box Sweet Reflections Dress Shop**

# Twinkle Twirl's Dance Studio

❑ **Twinkle Twirl** (stars and swirl)

    ❑ Tutu

    ❑ Vanity

    ❑ Punch bowl

    ❑ Ladle

    ❑ 5 desserts to place on the dessert stand

    ❑ 2 goblets

    ❑ Flower brush

**Mint in Box Twinkle Twirl's Dance Studio**

# Frilly Frocks Boutique

- ❐ **Frilly Frocks** (masquerade mask)
    - ❐ Sewing machine
    - ❐ Blue skirt
    - ❐ Pink skirt
    - ❐ 4 pink shoes
    - ❐ Crown
    - ❐ Glasses
    - ❐ Blue barrette
    - ❐ Blue necklace
    - ❐ Flower brush

**Exterior view of Frilly Frocks Boutique**

**Mint in Box Frilly Frocks Boutique**

# Rainbow Wishes Amusement Park

❑ **Round 'n Round** (Ferris wheel)
    ❑   Butterfly rollercoaster car
    ❑   Bow brush

**Mint in Box Rainbow Wishes Amusement Park**

# Wonder Waves Surf Shop

This set was first available exclusively at Sam's Club stores in the US, then spotted at Big Lots. It came with a new pony (Guava Lava) and three reissued ponies: Bowtie, Waterfire, and Strawberry Reef.

- ☐ **Guava Lava (**guava fruits and tropical drink)
- ☐ **Bowtie** (bows)
- ☐ **Waterfire** (flame and waves)
- ☐ **Strawberry Reef** (coral and strawberry)
  - ☐ Bathing suit
  - ☐ Bikini
  - ☐ Sunglasses
  - ☐ Snorkel mask
  - ☐ 4 flippers
  - ☐ Spinning storage rack
  - ☐ Surfboard
  - ☐ Radio
  - ☐ Sticker sheet
  - ☐ 4 Flower brushes

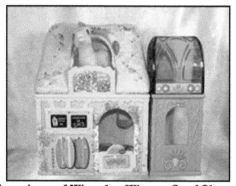

**Exterior view of Wonder Waves Surf Shop**

**Mint in box Wonder Waver Surf Shop**

# Butterfly Island Adventure

This playset contained the first baby Pegasus pony, Honolu-loo. Later, an edition of this playset was released exclusively at Costco stores containing a bonus pony, Anchors Away. A third edition of this playset was released exclusively at Toys R Us stores which included three bonus ponies: Waterfire, Ribbon Wishes, and Surf Star. Surf Star had been previously released as a bonus pony in the Seaside Celebration sets in other parts of the world, but this was her first appearance in the US.

❒ **Honolu-loo** (butterfly and flowers)

    ❒ Spinning clothes rack
    ❒ Palm tree
    ❒ Smoothie shack
    ❒ 2 signs
    ❒ Sandcastle mold
    ❒ Sandcastle
    ❒ Shovel
    ❒ Sand Pail
    ❒ Snorkel mask
    ❒ 4 flippers
    ❒ Grass skirt
    ❒ Brush

**Butterfly Island Adventure
(Costco exclusive edition)**
- ❏ **Anchor's Away** (anchor)

**Butterfly Island Adventure
(Toys R Us exclusive edition)**
- ❏ **Surf Star** (sailboat)
- ❏ **Waterfire** (flame and waves)
- ❏ **Ribbon Wishes** (star wand)

**Mint in box Butterfly Island Adventure
(Costco Exclusive Edition)**

**Butterfly Island Adventure
(Toys R Us Exclusive Edition)**

# Super Sundaes Ice Cream Parlor

The Super Sundaes Ice Cream Parlor was available exclusively at CVS Pharmacy stores during the 2005 holiday season.

- ☐ **Butterscotch** (lollipops)
- ☐ **Lickety Split** (sundae)
- ☐ **Cupcake** (cupcakes)
    - ☐ Soda counter
    - ☐ Cash register
    - ☐ Table
    - ☐ 3 Bow brushes

**Super Sundaes Ice Cream Shop exterior**

**Mint in Box Super Sundaes Ice Cream Shop**

# Twist and Style Petal Parlor

This playset was packaged with a bonus tiara that could hold the bonus jewels that were found in many of the Crystal Princess ponies that were released early in the year. Later, this set was packaged with a bonus Breezie, Snippity Snap, in some European countries.

- ☐ **Daffidazey** (cloth flower)
- ☐ **Zipzee** (flowers)
    - ☐ Flower platform
    - ☐ 3 barrettes
    - ☐ Tiara
    - ☐ Bow brush

☐ **Snippity Snap** (butterfly and dots)  ☐ **Zipzee** (flowers)

**Mint in Box Twist and Style Petal Parlor**

**Mint in Box Twist and Style Petal parlor with bonus crown.**

# Crystal Rainbow Castle

The Crystal Rainbow Castle could be "magically" opened using a magic wand. Initially, this playset was sold alone without any ponies, but during the holiday season, three new ponies were included as a bonus in a specially packaged set available at Wal-Mart stores. These ponies were not named on the packaging or on any inserts inside the package, but were named in an email from a Hasbro representative. They all have Fairytale themed symbols.

**Crystal Rainbow Castle**
- ❑ Wardrobe
- ❑ Table
- ❑ Vanity
- ❑ Punch bowl
- ❑ Punch ladle
- ❑ 2 goblets
- ❑ 2 ice cream dishes
- ❑ 2 spoons
- ❑ 3 canisters
- ❑ 3 perfume bottles

❏ **Pretty Palace** (damsel hat)

❏ **Crowning Glory** (crown on pillow)

❏ **Royal Beauty** (frog and heart)

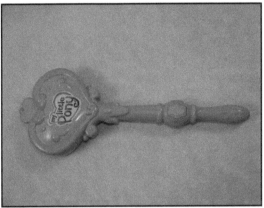

"Magic" Wand included in the bonus packaging used to open the castle

**Exterior view of Crystal Rainbow Castle**

**Mint in Box Crystal Rainbow Castle**

# Crystal Rainbow Accessory Sets

These sets were designed to allow you to decorate your Crystal Rainbow Castle.

**Crystal Rainbow Bedroom**
- ❒ Bed with drawer
- ❒ Tiara
- ❒ Blanket
- ❒ Pillow
- ❒ Sleeping mask
- ❒ Dresser
- ❒ 4 slippers

**Crystal Rainbow Dining Room**
- ❒ Table
- ❒ 4 placemats
- ❒ 6 desserts
- ❒ 4 cups
- ❒ 4 saucers
- ❒ Teapot

# Rainbow Princess Castle

This playset was only available overseas. The Rainbow Princess Castle uses the same basic design as the earlier Celebration Castle but is painted in pink with light purple trim. This set was also packaged with a short-haired Rarity which was not available for sale in the US.

*Picture of Rainbow Princess Castle provided by Linda Murphy

# Mail Order Pony Points Program

The Pony Points Program began in August of 2003. Special redemption points could be clipped from packages of My Little Pony merchandise and sent in with an order form for special products. A variety of things were offered including bracelets, playmates, videos, posters, and special ponies. Dazzle Surprise was the first pony to be offered through the Pony Points Program with Sunshimmer and Love Wishes replacing her later. In addition to the above-mentioned items, Hasbro added giant Frilly Frocks plush to its redemption form in December of 2004 through January of 2005. This item was very limited.

❑ **Dazzle Surprise** (confetti stars) (16 points)

❑ **Sunshimmer** (jeweled sun) (16 points)

❑ **Love Wishes** (love letters) (24 points)

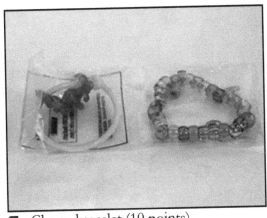

❑ Charm bracelet (10 points)
❑ Friendship bracelet (4 points)

❑ **Giant 3 ft tall Frilly Frocks Plush** (150 points)

### Additional Mail Order Items Offered:
❑ Playmat I (12 points)
❑ Charming Birthday video (8 points)
❑ Star Catcher poster (6 points)
❑ Playmat II (12 points)
❑ Butterfly Island poster (6 points)

# Disney Items

In 2004, four Disney Princess My Little Ponies were sold exclusively at Disney theme parks. These ponies were dressed as Disney Princesses and came packaged in special boxes decorated with Cinderella's Castle and Mickey Ears.

❏ **Pinkie Pie as Cinderella**
    ❏ Damsel hat
    ❏ Cape
    ❏ Tail ribbon
    ❏ Bow brush

❏ **Kimono as Belle**
    ❏ Damsel hat
    ❏ Cape
    ❏ Tail ribbon
    ❏ Bow brush

❏ **Sparkleworks as Aurora**
    ❏ Damsel hat
    ❏ Cape
    ❏ Tail ribbon
    ❏ Bow brush

❏ **Minty as Ariel**
    ❏ Damsel hat
    ❏ Cape
    ❏ Tail ribbon
    ❏ Bow brush

# Disney Build-a-Pony

Later that same year, the Build-a-Pony workshop opened at Disney's Once Upon a Toy store in Downtown Disney and later expanded to other areas in the parks. This station offered ponies and Disney themed accessories available for purchase. Shoppers could fill a box full of ponies and accessories for a fixed price regardless of the number of items. Ponies available included: Spring Parade, Golden Delicious, Piccolo, and Cinnamon Breeze.

In 2005, Build-a-Pony workshop added a Tinkerbell outfit, Minnie outfit, Mickey ears, a pink raincoat and hat with princess design (hat is not pictured), princess hat with Mickey ears, Mickey antennae (boppers), and Mickey sunglasses. In 2006, the workshop added additional costumes and accessories including the princess dresses from the set on the previous page as well as Snow White, Jasmine and new versions of Aurora, Cinderella, Ariel, and Belle.

# So Soft Baby Ponies

In 2004, So Soft Baby Ponies were available. They were large baby ponies with soft bodies and hard plastic faces. The first three So Soft ponies would giggle and make baby sounds when you squeezed them. They came with items like bottles, carriers, and brushes. In 2005, So Soft Baby ponies included dress-up outfits, themed accessories, and one even said a bedtime prayer. In early 2007, So Soft Newborn Ponies, Pinkie Pie and Rainbow Dash were available. Later releases of the So Soft Newborn Ponies contained bonus carriers.

- ☐ **Rose Blossom** (flower)
    - ☐ Pink bottle with pink trim
    - ☐ Pink carrier
    - ☐ Pink brush

- ☐ **Petal Blossom /Baby Alive** (butterfly)
    - ☐ Pink bottle with purple trim
    - ☐ Purple carrier
    - ☐ Purple brush

- ☐ **Pretty Powder TRU exclusive** (bow)
    - ☐ Pink bottle with magenta trim
    - ☐ Pink carrier
    - ☐ Head band
    - ☐ Magenta brush

- ☐ **Angel Dove** (bird, cloud, and hearts)
    - ☐ Tutu
    - ☐ Pink tiara
    - ☐ Purple brush

- ☐ **Junebug** (bug with flowers)
    - ☐ Yellow tiara with antenna
    - ☐ Wings
    - ☐ Pink brush

- ☐ **Misty Mornings Target Exclusive** (chick)
    - ☐ Skirt
    - ☐ Bonnet
    - ☐ Purple brush

❑ **Tripsy Daisy**
(bandage and flowers)
- ❑ Blue spoon
- ❑ Medicine bottle
- ❑ Thermometer
- ❑ Bandage
- ❑ Pink brush

❑ **Bon Appetite**
(bib and sippy cup)
- ❑ Sippy cup
- ❑ Food dish
- ❑ Blue spoon
- ❑ Bib
- ❑ Purple brush

❑ **Bright Night** (moon)
- ❑ Yellow brush

Good Morning Sunshine had electronic features that allowed the pony to lie down, talk, and open and close her eyes. A later release of Good Morning Sunshine contained a bonus Sweetsong mini plush.

❑ **Good Morning Sunshine**
(smiling sun and clouds)
- ❑ Pacifier
- ❑ Yellow bottle with pink top
- ❑ Pink brush

❑ **Soakey Dokey**
- ❑ Frog towel
- ❑ Bath toy
- ❑ Pink brush

❑ **So Soft Newborn Pinkie Pie**
- ❑ Bottle

❑ **So Soft Newborn Rainbow Dash**
- ❑ Pacifier

# Ponyville

During the 2006 Christmas season, Hasbro began to release a new line of miniature My Little Ponies under the name Ponyville. These mini ponies were sold individually, in sets, and with playsets.

This set was only available for a short time during the 2006 holiday season but was later re-leased in a Ponyville Holiday tube.

- ☐ **Pinkie Pie**
- ☐ **Sparkleworks**
- ☐ **Minty**
- ☐ **Wysteria**
    - ☐ 4 Santa socks
    - ☐ Santa hat

This set was exclusive to Target stores during the Valentine's Day Season.

- ☐ **Valenshy**
- ☐ **Wish-I-May**
- ☐ **Always & Forever**
    - ☐ Ice cream soda
    - ☐ Plate of cookies
    - ☐ Teddy bear

- ☐ **Yours Truly**
- ☐ **Wish-I-Might**
- ☐ **Fantastical February**
    - ☐ Hair bow
    - ☐ Perfume bottle
    - ☐ Plate of cupcakes

This set was exclusive to Target stores during the Valentine's Day Season.

**Meet for Ice Cream with Triple Treat**
- ☐ **Triple Treat**
    - ☐ Ice cream cart
    - ☐ Butterfly
    - ☐ Visor
    - ☐ 4 Ice cream treats

**Swing Along with Sunny Daze**
- ❑ **Sunny Daze**
    - ❑ Swing
    - ❑ Bird
    - ❑ Sun hat
    - ❑ 2 flower bouquets

**Birthday Afternoon with Rainbow Dash & Bunches-O-Fun**
- ❑ **Rainbow Dash**
- ❑ **Bunches-O-Fun**
    - ❑ Table with balloon
    - ❑ Birthday cake
    - ❑ Punch bowl
    - ❑ Punch ladle
    - ❑ 2 cups
    - ❑ Pizza box with pizza
    - ❑ 2 gift boxes
    - ❑ Teddy bear
    - ❑ 2 pieces of cake on plates
    - ❑ 2 ice cream sundaes
    - ❑ 2 lollipops
    - ❑ 2 party hats

**Fancy Fashions with Desert Rose & Sew-and-So**
- [ ] **Desert Rose**
- [ ] **Sew-and-So**
    - [ ] Vanity
    - [ ] Coat hanger
    - [ ] 4 skirts
    - [ ] 2 wings
    - [ ] 4 sets of 4 shoes
- [ ] Hair dryer
- [ ] Perfume bottle
- [ ] 2 hair bows
- [ ] Hair brush

**Scootin' Along with Scooter Sprite & Daisy Jo**
- [ ] **Scooter Sprite**
- [ ] **Daisy Jo**
    - [ ] 2 scooters
    - [ ] Bunny
    - [ ] Umbrella
    - [ ] 2 helmets
- [ ] 2 backpacks
- [ ] 2 water bottles
- [ ] 2 daisies

**A Very Minty Christmas Tree**

❏ **Minty**
   ❏ Cookie tray
   ❏ 2 mugs of hot coco

Exterior view of A Very Minty
Christmas Tree

Mint in box A Very Minty
Christmas Tree

## Sweet Shoppe

☐ **Sweetberry**

☐ Counter  ☐ 2 ice cream cones

☐ Table  ☐ 2 ice cream sodas

☐ Easel  ☐ 3 deserts

☐ Freezer  ☐ Menu

☐ 2 lollipops  ☐ Mail

Exterior view of Sweet Shoppe

Mint in box Sweet Shoppe

**Pinkie Pie's Balloon House**

- ❐ **Pinkie Pie**
- ❐ **Blossomforth**
    - ❐ Bed
    - ❐ Table
    - ❐ Seesaw
    - ❐ Frog
    - ❐ Vase
- ❐ Flower
- ❐ 2 Perfume bottles
- ❐ Bath brush
- ❐ 2 sandwiches on plates
- ❐ 2 cups
- ❐ Mail

This set was also available at Toys R Us stores with bonus Fair Weather and Magic Marigold ponies and a bonus scooter.

- ❐ **Fair Weather**
- ❐ **Magic Marigold**
    - ❐ Scooter
    - ❐ Helmet

These ponies and accessories were included in bonus packages available at Toys R Us stores.

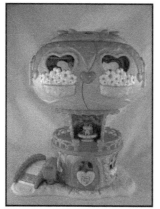

Exterior view of Pinkie Pie's Balloon House

Mint in box Pinkie Pie's Balloon House

Mint in box Pinkie Pie's Balloon House with bonus ponies

# Yarn Hair Plush

Hasbro introduced soft and cuddly plush ponies with yarn hair. The first three (Rainbow Dash, Tink-a-Tink-a-Too, and Pinkie Pie) were available in 2004. The others shown were available in 2005.

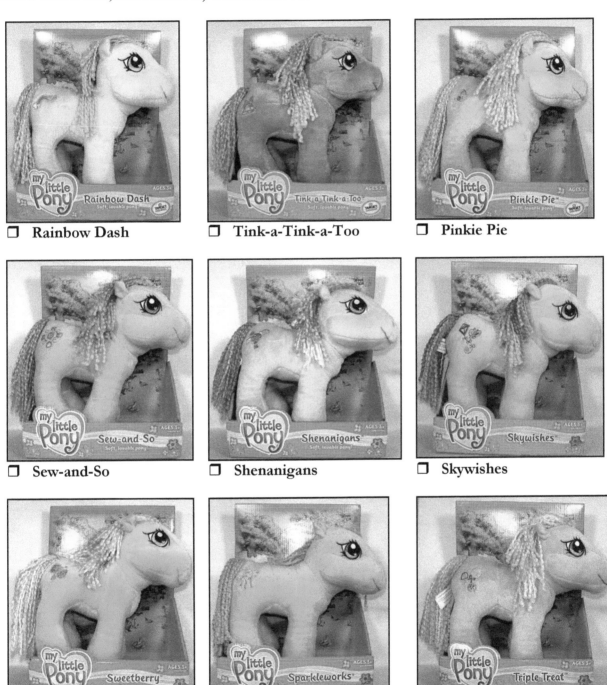

❒ **Rainbow Dash**  ❒ **Tink-a-Tink-a-Too**  ❒ **Pinkie Pie**

❒ **Sew-and-So**  ❒ **Shenanigans**  ❒ **Skywishes**

❒ **Sweetberry**  ❒ **Sparkleworks**  ❒ **Triple Treat**

❏ **Singing Minty**

Singing Minty was available during the 2005 holiday season. When you squeeze her she sings a song from the My Little Pony movie, A Very Minty Christmas. A pre-release Singing Minty was also available as part of a raffle at the My Little Pony Fair during the summer of 2005.

Three Yarn Hair Plush Ponies were available exclusively at My Little Pony Live shows. They differ from earlier releases by display side as well as by having "My Little Pony Live" printed on their front hoof.

❏ **Pinkie Pie**

❏ **Sweetberry**

❏ **Sew-and-So**

Close-up of printed hoof

# Tiny Tins

Tiny Tins ponies were small molded ponies with jointed necks. They came packaged with a decorative collectible tin. Two sets of six ponies were available.

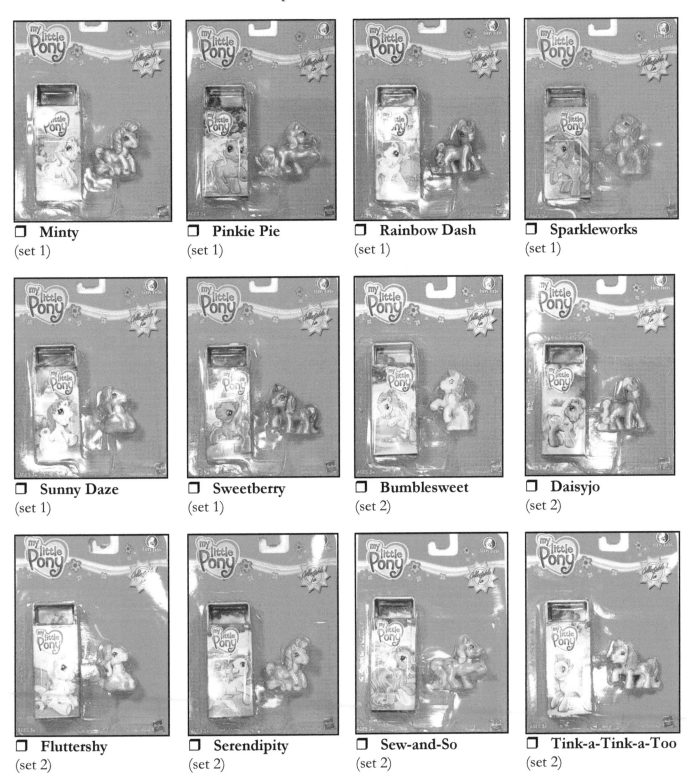

❏ **Minty**
(set 1)

❏ **Pinkie Pie**
(set 1)

❏ **Rainbow Dash**
(set 1)

❏ **Sparkleworks**
(set 1)

❏ **Sunny Daze**
(set 1)

❏ **Sweetberry**
(set 1)

❏ **Bumblesweet**
(set 2)

❏ **Daisyjo**
(set 2)

❏ **Fluttershy**
(set 2)

❏ **Serendipity**
(set 2)

❏ **Sew-and-So**
(set 2)

❏ **Tink-a-Tink-a-Too**
(set 2)

# McDonald's Ponies

In 2005, McDonald's restaurants offered My Little Pony toys in their happy meals. A set of eight was available in the US and Canada. Each pony in this set came with an accessory. In Europe, a different set of four ponies was available.

**US and Canada Happy Meal Ponies**
Top row: Sparkleworks, Butterscotch, Wysteria
Middle row: Daisy Jo, Serendipity, Starswirl
Front row: Minty, Pinkie Pie

**Europe Happy Meal Ponies**
Top row: Cloud Dancer, Star Dancer
Front row: Spring Treat, Star Bright

**Happy Meal box from the Netherlands**

# Brazilian G3 Ponies

In 2005, Hasbro licensed toymaker Candide to produce My Little Pony toys. These ponies were unlike any that had been produced previously.

❏ **Large Green Baby**
(Rainbow Dash's symbol)
    ❏ Purple brush
    ❏ Green comb

❏ **Large Pink Baby**
(Rainbow Dash's symbol)
    ❏ Pink brush
    ❏ Purple comb

❏ **Green Sitting Minty**
(Minty's symbol)

❏ **Purple Sitting Minty**
(Minty's symbol)

❏ **Pink Walking Sunny Daze** (sun)

❏ **Yellow Walking Sunny Daze** (sun)

❏ **No Symbol Rainbow Dash**

❏ **No Symbol Minty**

❏ **No Symbol Pinkie Pie**

❏ **No Symbol Sunny Daze**

❏ **No Symbol Sunny Daze**

# Mexican G3 Ponies

In 2007, Grocery Outlet stores in the US carried a series of different G3 ponies. The packages contain Spanish writing. These ponies are very similar to the Brazil G3 ponies in size. Small ponies were packaged both with bed or kitchen accessories as well as in small plastic containers. All small ponies were also available in two different poses. A two pack with Rarity and Royal Bouquet in the same pose as Brazilian walking Sunny Daze was also available, but is not pictured.

❐ **Large Baby Minty**
   ❐ Purple brush
   ❐ Pink comb

❐ **Large Baby Desert Rose**
   ❐ Pink brush
   ❐ Purple comb

❐ **Rarity**

❐ **Royal Bouquet**

❐ **Desert Rose**

❐ **Minty**

# Index of Pony Names

No matter which generation of MLP you collect, Priced Nostalgia Press has you covered! For more info about any of the books below, visit us online at http://www.mylittleponycollecting.com

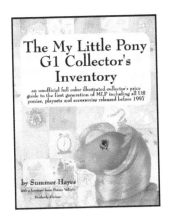

## The My Little Pony G1 Collector's Inventory

By Summer Hayes
ISBN: 9780978606312
A full color, illustrated price guide to the playsets, accessories and ponies released before 1997

## The My Little Pony G2 Collector's Inventory

By Summer Hayes
ISBN: 9780978606329
A full color, illustrated price guide to the playsets, accessories and ponies released from 1997 to 2003

## The My Little Pony G3 Collector's Inventory

By Summer Hayes
ISBN: 9780978606350
A full color, illustrated guide to the playsets, accessories and ponies released from 2003 to 2007

## The My Little Pony 2007-2008 Collector's Inventory

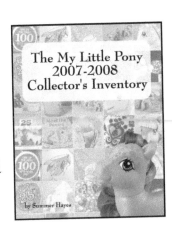

By Summer Hayes
ISBN: 978-0978606367
A full color, illustrated guide to the playsets, accessories and ponies released from 2007 to 2008 that picks up where *The My Little Pony G3 Collector's Inventory* left off

Lightning Source UK Ltd.
Milton Keynes UK
UKHW052121060920
369447UK00006B/39